A Boy Grows in Brooklyn

A Boy Grows in Brooklyn

An Educational and Spiritual Memoir

ROBERT W. PAZMIÑO

WIPF & STOCK · Eugene, Oregon

A BOY GROWS IN BROOKLYN
An Educational and Spiritual Memoir

Wipf & Stock
An Imprint of Wipf and Stock Publishers
199 W. 8th Ave., Suite 3
Eugene, OR 97401

www.wipfandstock.com

ISBN 13: 978–1-62564–658-3

Manufactured in the U.S.A.   05/27/2014

Dedicated to my grandchildren,

Oliver Albert and Eli Theodore Pazmiño

Contents

Introduction
The Manna of Memories

ach person's life is a story with fascinating twists and turns representing a tapestry of formative educational influences. My life story unfolded in Brooklyn, New York, where millions of lives have been launched over the years. I was born on June 15, 1948 with a family lineage others have observed is only possible in a global city like New York: my father is Ecuadorean and my mother is a mix of Dutch and German. When I shared this diverse background with my high school junior English class, one peer shouted out "Bingo," to note the distinct mix as compared with others. Brooklyn was known as the borough of churches and my life pursuit of a religious profession was no doubt influenced by the local church my family and I attended each week—Kenilworth Baptist Church, located just one block from our apartment building at 2620 Glenwood Road, between East 26th and 27th streets and in full view of Flatbush Avenue, Brooklyn's main thoroughfare.

One of the etchings I commonly found in the boy's bathroom of the Brooklyn public schools I attended (Public School 152, Andries Hudde Junior High School, and Midwood High School), was "Jesus saves, but Moses invests." As a Gentile growing up in the predominantly Jewish neighborhood of Flatbush now known as Midwood, I learned to appreciate different perspectives on life and religious faith. A Jewish perspective is certainly reflected in the title of this introduction, "The Manna of Memories." And I always wondered about my friends' and neighbors' celebration of Passover, the account of which I had discovered in my Protestant Bible. The mixed crowds of people (Exodus 12:38) and slaves whom God delivered from Egypt were miraculously sustained in their unbelievable forty-year journey through God's provision of manna gathered each morning with a double portion before the Sabbath day of rest. With the passing years of middle age, I realize that my memories of Brooklyn boyhood serve to sustain me as I pass on stories to my grandchildren and make connections with the wonder of everyday life in our postmodern age. The clarity of the long-term memories in the accounts of nursing home residents where my mother-in-law resided for three years in Florida and now two years in nearby Weston, may well represent the double portion of manna as they prepare for their final Sabbath rest in a life to come.

My Brooklyn boyhood and adolescence is a journey worth passing on from the perspective of a current-day, Hispanic, North American professor of Christian education, who relishes sharing how life in a hyphenated world is worth celebrating. My life, as I imagine each person's life, is sustained daily by a steady stream of memories that serve to maintain the continuities of human existence with meaning, joy, and on occasion lament. With the aging process marred by dementia for some, like my mother and mother-in-law, life's meaning is salvaged with vignettes of long-term memories of noteworthy incidents that serve to define who we are. One's memories provide glimpses of the gift of life and the tapestry of the generations.

Memories are ever-present vestiges of the past that can invite the celebration of life's gifts worth passing on to the rising generations. Museums, like the Brooklyn Museum that I visited weekly in junior high with my buddy George Marmorino to pick up slides for the following week's social studies class, also house the vestiges of our past in an amazing variety of forms. Brooklyn Museum actually houses replica rooms from earlier historical periods. Our own life stories provide museum legacies of sorts that we can pass onto others and provide perspective for the common journeys we share. My memoir represents one written replica filtered through years of work and thought as an educator fascinated by what we learn and, in turn, can teach others.

One hope I have in writing my memoir is to pass onto my children and grandchildren accounts to delight their hearts, as well as lessons to accompany their personal journeys. Such accounts are most often shared orally, but now have been transcribed in writing to create a more lasting form. The entries comprising my educational memoir represent a yearning to pass on long-lasting precious items, much like the gold, silver, and precious gems the fleeing Israelites received from the grieving Egyptians. Those items were both used to adorn the tabernacle of communal worship, and to construct the golden calf, which shows that receiving a legacy requires its discerning use.

Growing up in a predominantly Jewish neighborhood meant I imbibed a life that celebrated the importance of education. Learning was highly valued and I competed academically with many others in striving for excellence in thought and work. Over time this striving for excellence was associated with loving God with all of one's mind. This love was actually commanded in both the Jewish and Christian Scriptures. I learned not only in schools, but in all of life's relationships and experiences.

Therefore, my memoir is organized to highlight the key educational roles that family, school, the church, the local community, peers, scouting programs, media, and the wider society played in my formation as a boy. I begin with the context of Brooklyn itself that served as the local community within which I grew. Brooklyn is a borough where two and a half million people currently live, including my daughter. The memories do not, however, always stay within neat institutional categories because life itself involves the complex intersections and concurrent ebbs and flows of the various sectors of everyday existence. The interplay creates the tapestry of our individual journeys. Lessons learned from this interplay are shared, creating manna that sustains my life and its legacy to pass on. Memories frame our perceptions and connections in life. William Wordsworth in his poem "My Heart Leaps Up When I Behold" from his collected work *Ode: Intimations of Immortality* observed "The child is the father of the man." His observation holds some truth for my life.

Special thanks are owed to my daughter Rebekah Joy who served as the careful initial editor of this work. She is a gifted writer who currently uses her skills in writing legal briefs as an appellate criminal defense attorney. Richard Dutton who shares my Brooklyn roots and similar memories also provided valuable editorial support. I am also indebted to my other family members who read and responded to drafts of this memoir supporting my effort to pass on a living legacy for generations to come. Special appreciation is owed to the Wabash Center for Teaching and Learning who supported my memoir writing with a grant, to participants in the Wabash Mid-Career Theological Faculty Colloquium (2010–2011) as we explored the arts together, and to Ronald B. Schwartz who was my instructor in a memoir writing class offered through Newton Community Education.

Dr. Elizabeth Conde-Frazier, a dear colleague whom I have mentored in the past, has graciously written about my life and contributions to Christian education for the on-line project "Christian Educators of the Twentieth Century" and her entry can be accessed at http://www.talbot.edu/ce20/educators/protestant/robert_pazmino/.

1

Community

BRING THE BUMS BACK TO BROOKLYN

The Brooklyn Dodgers were the baseball heroes of my boyhood and their long-suffering fans were finally rewarded with their only World Series win in 1955. When they won, my friends and I joined the celebrating crowds, pulling our wagons right down the center line of Brooklyn's busy main thoroughfare, Flatbush Avenue, stopping all traffic in our victory procession.

The 1955 Dodgers roster included Gil Hodges at first base, whom I met years later in person, Junior Gilliam at second, Pee Wee Reese at short stop, Jackie Robinson at third, Sandy Amoros in left field, Duke Snider in center, Carl Furillo at right, and Roy Campanella behind the plate. Starting pitchers whose names I recall are Don Newcombe and Johnny Podres, with the young fireball, left-hander Sandy Koufax in the bull pen. The Brooklyn Dodgers held a particular fascination for me because I went with my dad to Ebbets Field, the shrine of our borough, to watch them play. My dad played in his early years with a semi-pro team, the Flatbush Dodgers. On special occasions he would thrill me with accounts of his escapades with the hapless Flatbush Dodgers, their travels, and their games in the metropolitan area and even upstate and out of state.

Baseball loyalties and rivalries ran deep across New York City and its five boroughs during the fifties, heightened by "subway series" that pitted the ever-winning and star-studded Yankees, the Bronx bombers, against either the Manhattan-based Giants or hapless Dodgers from Brooklyn. A team from Queens would have to await the Mets in later years and Staten Island never fielded a professional team.

The Dodgers, better known to their fans as the "Bums," always managed to lose to either the New York Giants in the National League Championships or to the hated New York Yankees in the World Series. Nonetheless, those motley Dodgers represented for me a cultural and racial mix of loveable characters who modeled the diversity of my home town. It was not just Jackie Robinson on the regular team roster who broke baseball's racial barrier, but Roy Campanella, Sandy Amoros, and Junior Gilliam were also African American and starters. Sandy Koufax was Jewish and held great promise controlling that amazing fastball. If men from such diverse backgrounds could contribute on the national baseball scene, perhaps, just perhaps there was hope for a bicultural boy to make a contribution in life, even if baseball was not my chosen game. Of course, soon after their series win the Dodgers betrayed their loyal fans and went off into exile in Los Angeles. There is always the persistent hope that someday they will return. One of my faculty colleagues with whom I team taught a course on teaching the Bible, Bill Herzog, co-edited a work on baseball entitled *Baseball: The Faith of Fifty Million: Baseball, Religion and American Culture*. Baseball took on the quality of a civil religion for Brooklynites.

Now what about my life-changing meeting with Gil Hodges? Gil had the special knack of hitting a timely grand slam homerun that would often reverse the Dodgers' fortunes in a closely contested game. I never imagined I'd meet Gil, whom I saw so many times at Ebbets Field. During the summer of 1968, between my sophomore and junior years in college, I was employed as a teller by the

Chase Manhattan Bank at a very busy branch on Nostrand Avenue and Kings Highway. The branch was in walking distance of Marine Park fields where I practiced baseball with my dad and friends. In teller's school I had received the highest scores on our final tests before we were commissioned to one of the local branches located in the five boroughs of New York. I counted myself blessed to be placed in a Brooklyn branch—an easy bus ride from my home and just a few blocks from where I attended Andries Hudde Junior High School.

Upon arriving at the Chase bank branch I was informed by co-workers that this very branch was where the former Dodger great Gil Hodges and his wife did their personal banking. One younger, sassy, and attractive blond teller warned me, "Just wait until you meet Mrs. Hodges!" Thinking only of the celebrity image of baseball fame, I questioned her words and longed for meeting the Hodges family and serving their banking needs as meticulously instructed in teller's school. My high teller school grades failed me when for the first three weeks of heavy branch service I did not balance out most days. That fact increasingly became the concern of my branch manager who noticed that the head teller was also having problems tallying up. I suppose suspicion increased when my co-workers learned of my upcoming engagement, which required saving up for a diamond ring. Scrutiny of my less than stellar performance was only diverted when Mrs. Hodges did actually appear at the branch.

It was a slow, late morning in mid-week when Mrs. Hodges drove up to the drive-in teller's window in her sleek car. The same sassy teller who warned me was providentially in position to serve her, but Mrs. Hodges was wearing sunglasses and a wide brim hat. Once the teller asked for Mrs. Hodges' identification, all hell broke loose and my fellow tellers and I challenged to keep our laughter under wraps. We could all hear Mrs. Hodges' protest over the teller's speaker about not being instantly recognized.

My colleague added insult to injury when she turned away from the window and shared with all of us her response: "How the hell am I to recognize her? She is not wearing a Dodger's cap!" Not knowing she failed to shut off the customer's speaker, the teller all too soon learned that Mrs. Hodges heard her.

At that point Mrs. Hodges was enraged. She left her car in the drive-up teller's lane after slamming its door and rushed into the branch. She vented all her frustration and threats upon our ever-diligent branch manager, Mr. Russo. Relieved from the manger's scrutiny, I began to prove myself with a balanced ledger at the end of most business days.

My encounter with Mrs. Hodges' better half came on a busy Friday afternoon when my co-workers alerted me that Gil himself had in fact entered the branch. He chose my line out of four possible ones. Once he arrived at my window, with my mouth agape and mesmerized at his height, I heard Gil ask me to cash his check. I had learned at that point not to ask him for identification, but I was so overwhelmed by the amount of the check that I failed to survey if there were more in the pile.

After cashing the first check Gil graciously observed, "Son, I think there is more." Fumbling, I somehow managed to discover a second check and proceeded to also cash its large amount, and then felt relieved. Relieved until Gil's next response, "Son, there is still more!" Embarrassed and still in a daze, I finally managed to see and cash all four checks and was very appreciative of Gil's patience as compared with his wife's memorable tirade.

Over those summer weeks of banking I somehow managed to give away to one business courier an extra $800 in cash. He graciously returned half of that amount. My rationalization did not please the bank manager and after a week-long special bank audit that he requested, I had a fateful meeting.

Mr. Russo said, "Robert, we like you as a fine person. But we cannot afford to keep you this summer. Since you arrived, Janet has also has problems in her head teller work. We even had a local branch audit. I did check with the Manhattan downtown main office and nothing else is available for summer work. You might spend more time at the beach before college begins again."

I was fired from that branch and exiled from banking. Like the bums who left Brooklyn, I left the prospects of a business career assured of having more interest in the people I met than the business I transacted or honestly, did not successfully transact.

For the past thirty years I have lived in Massachusetts. Someday I might return to Brooklyn as my wife and I consider retirement plans. My daughter wears a t-shirt with the logo "Bring the Dodgers Back to Brooklyn." To this I reply "Amen!"

Plans are for the New Jersey Nets to come to Brooklyn and not for the Dodgers to return, which the Nets did in 2012. Actually basketball is favored to baseball in most Brooklyn neighborhoods these days.

Lessons Learned

Role models are important for growing up and often sports celebrities serve as those models, provided we recognize their humanity. Sport teams also contribute to a sense of community spirit that transcends our cultural, racial, and ethnic differences.

BEDFORD AVENUE DIVIDE AND BORDER CROSSING

My life in an apartment house on Glenwood Road gradually distinguished itself from those who lived on the west side of Bedford Avenue divide. Apartment living was very different from life in private homes. Apartment living meant I had ready-made friends on each of the six floors of 2620, with each apartment housing a wide diversity of folk. Ordinary lives took on extraordinary qualities for a boy becoming acquainted with families and individuals different from me. Though different, all those folk were not viewed as deficient because they were all welcome into our apartment, and they were often present for shared meals.

Bedford Avenue divided those whose who could afford a private home from those who could not. There were a few exceptions among friends on my side of Bedford, including Charlie Prado whose parents came from Spain. He lived in a small house on Kenilworth Place. We often gathered at Charlie's house because both his parents worked, affording us certain freedoms. Bobby Friedman was part of my circle of friends. He was the other exception, living in a large house just down the block from Charlie. His dad was a doctor and we rarely went to his house, which included his dad's office. Charlie later in life became a professional lifeguard living in Hawaii, but Bobby was always the rebel.

Will Herberg wrote *Protestant, Catholic, Jew* in 1955 to describe the American religious landscape of my boyhood. My apartment house and neighborhood reversed that national order and could be described as *Jew, Catholic, Protestant* to capture its proportional religious makeup. I grew up a decided minority in a predominantly Jewish neighborhood and among Christians, a standout Protestant among Catholic friends, including John Reily of Irish descent, Charlie with Spaniard roots, and Douglas Curtis who was Italian. Curtis' dad changed his Italian name to be more acceptable. The one exception to my local minority religious status came on Brooklyn Day when the Sunday Schools of "the borough of churches" paraded down Bedford Avenue with floats and bands in a public display of our religious and communal diversity.

I intentionally made friends with boys from the other side of Bedford and in a few cases sought to know girls as well from that side of the neighborhood. In fourth and fifth grades I had a crush on Carol Schwartz, whom I discovered lived beyond Bedford and even Ocean Avenue going west from East 26th Street. I would often ride my bike past her huge house hoping to catch a glance of her in her windows. In school I would often doodle the letters on top of each other that spelled out "I LOVE CAROL" in a secret acrostic known only to my young heart.

Many years later, I learned to my great embarrassment that Carol had observed my longing bike rides around her house. I was an elementary school stalker. Carol had long dark blonde hair that I longed to touch and a beautiful face with a shy and retiring personality. But Carol never returned to P. S. 152 for sixth grade, likely swept off to private school.

My affections in sixth grade soon shifted to Kathy Mankes who shared my budding amorous interests, but always at a safe distance. Serendipitously and partly by my design, I met Kathy's brother Seth at afterschool activities. I wisely befriended him even though he was only a fifth grader. This friendship enabled frequent visits to Seth's home on the better side of Bedford and special glimpses and encounters with Kathy when she was home. Kathy and Seth's family were Jewish and mine was not. One day Seth directly warned me that I could never be Kathy's boyfriend because of the religious divide.

After elementary school, I never saw Seth again until my first day at Midwood High School in September 1963. At a gathering of all those students selected to participate in the special math and science honors program, he spied me out. Whereas I had taken the three-year special program in junior high, Seth had taken the special two-year program at Midwood's Annex school of Kensington. So we were in the same tenth grade program.

Seth later became student "Mayor of the City of Midwood" and President of the Student Council. "City" yes, because there were 893 students alone in my graduating class in 1966. This indicated Seth's leadership role in a large urban high school that had staggered three-session days just to accommodate all the sophomore, junior, and senior students. Midwood occupied a full city block on Bedford Avenue across the street from the Brooklyn College campus on its south side.

Seth, now taller than me, queried: "What are you doing here, Paz [my nickname]?"

He had never anticipated that a Gentile from the wrong side of Bedford Avenue with the reputation of being tough and an athlete could manage being in such a competitive and selective program.

"I am here to study," was my response to his startled and dumbfounded stare.

It was abundantly clear in adolescence that the religious and class divide should not be crossed by expressing affection, especially to Seth's sister, or any Jewish girl for that matter.

Nevertheless, in kindergarten I did kiss my classmate while on top of the monkey bars. She may have been Jewish, but more likely Italian. I could not tell at that age. My best recollection is that the peck on the lips was mutually satisfying, even if a taboo in later elementary grades, except for spin-the-bottle games at coed parties in fifth and sixth grades.

While having an interest in girls and the wonder of their bodies, my primary energies focused on school, sports, scouts, family, and church life with little time and no significant resources to invest in dating the opposite sex. Interest was present, but not the opportunity.

Summer camp was another matter in that my last years of high school provided the opportunity to express interest in young women. I even met one beautiful young woman who resembled the film star Natalie Wood. That woman, Wanda Ruth Melendez eventually became my wife in 1969.

We met the summer of 1966 when we were both camp counselors at Metropolitan Baptist Camps in Poughquag, New York. This was the summer after my senior year in high school and just before heading off to Bucknell University located in Lewisburg, Pennsylvania. Wanda was headed to Ottawa University in Kansas.

Wanda's ethnic roots were Puerto Rican and her mom was a college graduate who worked as a social worker for New York City's Child Welfare Department. Wanda lived with her mom and her brother Omar in the Soundview area of the Bronx at 1219 Rosedale Avenue. Her parents were divorced and she had grown up in East Harlem in Manhattan with a three-year residence in Puerto Rico during her junior high years. Wanda was also Baptist and spoke of her "personal relationship with Jesus Christ" in her life. This was new language for me, as I came from a more liberal Protestant tradition, but my interest was piqued and reinforced with the messages shared by Pastor Bob Santilli who visited the camp. He spoke of the need to own one's faith and to make a life commitment to follow Christ as a disciple throughout one's life. I struggled with what this all meant, but near the end of the summer had a dramatic faith encounter.

During counselor orientation that summer I attempted to welcome all newcomers to the camp. While being attracted to Wanda and offering to her the wisdom from my previous summers experience, she surprisingly said to me, "You know, I don't like you."

I said, "Okay" and quickly backed off.

You can imagine my reluctance to learn the next day that Wanda and I were the two counselors selected to oversee the junior and senior high area together. I had just graduated from high school and Wanda the year before. She had worked for a year at New York Life Insurance Company while attending Hunter College at night.

I offered a peaceful gesture, "Wanda, though you don't like me, I hope we work well together with our campers."

Three weeks later when Wanda and I were walking back to our area after late afternoon swimming in the lake, a cold wind rushed through the trees and chilled us all. I quickly volunteered my services to keep her warm by placing my arm around her shoulder as we walked the long path back to our platform tents. I ventured a peck on her lips that was well received. Our romance quickly flourished that summer and led me to call my parents the next weekend directly informing them:

"Mom and Dad, I have met the girl I want to marry."

I shocked them because I had not dated during high school and the very next weekend the family visited camp to meet my beloved Wanda. They took us out of the camp for a meal at a nearby restaurant, but en route my younger siblings recall to this day saying:

"Bobby is kissing her again!"

The very next weekend we were back in the city on counselors' break, both Wanda's and my extended families met in her Bronx apartment. Her mom prepared a delicious meal, and my cousin Joseph and Uncle Victor also attended to seal the deal. Wanda's family was Puerto Rican, so Spanish was spoken some of our time together.

At summer's end, Wanda and I were sitting alone in Pell Lodge at the camp before a huge stone fireplace that had a hand-carved wooden cross displayed on its mantle. Wanda and I were headed off to college in a few weeks to Kansas and Pennsylvania.

In focusing on the cross I realized that Jesus' life and death offered to me a gift and new life requiring my response of faith. I recognized my need for sins forgiven and God's gracious provision of a remedy in Jesus Christ's willing death upon the cross. God's love in Christ called for a response of my love and life commitment. In this faith commitment I was crossing the borders of mainline Protestant life into evangelical faith, and in meeting Wanda and her extended family entered into the unknown Puerto Rican community that welcomed me with open arms during our two-year courting, one-year engagement in 1968, and eventual marriage on August 16, 1969. That date was also the historic Woodstock event, but we were wed in East Harlem at the Second Spanish Baptist Church on a hazy, ninety-five-degree day. With a traffic delay from Wanda's home in the Bronx to Manhattan along Bruckner Boulevard, she arrived forty-five minutes late. In the heat I lost five pounds, but the long ordeal was worth the wait as we launched our married life together the summer before my senior year.

Lessons Learned

Crossing borders requires navigating skills for dealing positively with differences. Quick judgments can lead to misunderstanding and lost opportunities for life-changing connections. Divisions are most tested with potential amorous relationships, as was the case for Romeo and Juliet about whom I read in junior high.

NEIGHBORHOOD BULLYING

Fears are a part of every childhood, some real and others imagined. Life on the city streets of Brooklyn presented its challenges for those who ventured beyond one's apartment to play with peers.

Play areas included sidewalks, alley ways between apartment houses, basements, roofs, a nearby college campus, school yards, city play grounds, city streets while dodging traffic, a beach within a bus ride, and, in my case, a nearby safety zone at the intersection of streets that met at an angle, which was ideal.

The safety zone sat in the shadow of the triangular apartment house that stood at the intersection of East 27th Street and Amersfort Place. The zone became a handy punch ball or even softball diamond, even though it was narrow and there was danger of hitting one of the many windows in the building. Play on the streets could be rough and tumble and not welcome for the faint-hearted.

My introduction to the dangers of street play came when I was just five years old and living on the second floor apartment, 2E, of 2620 Glenwood Road. That apartment could be reached easiest by taking the one stairway that led off to the right from the lobby accessed through two heavy entrance doors decorated with thick glass and fancy grillwork. Upon entering the building, there was also an elevator that served all six floors and a second stairway directly ahead of the front entrance. But when speed was of the essence, the right staircase was the safest and quickest route home.

It was a sunny summer day that invited adventure. I dressed myself in my favorite play shorts, striped t-shirt and well-worn blue sneakers. Blue was, and still is, my favorite color. One never knew who might be outside, but with so many children living in the four six-story apartment buildings just on my block, playmates were in ready supply.

I walked out the front entrance with no children in sight. We would usually play stoop ball right there in the alcove, set back from the wide sidewalk in front of our building. I wondered, "Where could everyone be?"

When I reached the sidewalk along Glenwood, no one could be seen. This was odd, so I ventured to East 27th Street and peered around the corner.

My efforts were not in vain. Clustered on the steps that led directly to the first floor doctor's office was a large group of children of all ages and something had them riled up. It was obvious from their loud talking.

I had to find out what was happening. I quickly learned that something was stolen from the steps where a girl had left them while playing hopscotch. It was her money, saved hidden in a tissue for the Good Humor ice cream man's visit that afternoon. She had wanted to treat her friends, and all were very disappointed and in search of the thief.

One of the older boys spied me joining the group and accused me of taking the money.

"No, no" I protested. "I just came out and didn't take it. Someone else did it!" I shouted to no avail.

"No, you did it because I saw you," replied my accuser supported by the mob of children ready to exact their justice.

I was to be the scapegoat and was pushed hard in my chest by that older boy, demanding that I return the money that I must have taken upstairs to my apartment. Surrounded by my accusers, my only option was somehow to push through them all and run for home.

Good thing I was a fast runner, but the older boys were soon at my heels as I dashed around the corner to my building and through the front doors. I ran straight to the right stairway, just in advance of their pursuit, taking two stairs at a time holding onto the railing for my life.

Fortunately my apartment door was unlocked and I rushed in trembling and out of breath. I quickly locked the door behind me ignoring the door banging that accompanied my daring escape. My mom must have gone up to the roof to hang the laundry with my older sister, so I had to face the mob alone. On the spot I decided to take the matter into my own hands and confront my false accuser. My small wooden bat would avenge the real threat. With my bat retrieved from under my bed, I listened at the door to make sure my pursuers had left the hallway. I carefully descended to the first floor lobby, which was all clear.

I girded up my courage and ran out the entrance and around the corner with my bat held high. When the mob saw me approaching, while I was proclaiming my innocence, all began to run. My focus and speed were upon my accuser who had pushed and threatened me. He had bullied me in the past and I had enough.

Half way up the block, I caught up with him and hit him squarely on the back of his head. He kept running and I turned to confront any remaining accusers. None were to be seen as they witnessed my speedy counter attack.

I had overcome my fears and felt vindicated. Vindicated, until the next day when my accuser's mom met up with me and recounted how her son had to see the doctor from my timely blow.

"I am sorry, but he lied," was my response.

My neighborhood reputation followed that incident and the usual local bullies avoided contact with me. I do regret resorting to violence in resolving conflict, but fears of other threats kept me diligent when playing on Brooklyn streets.

Lessons Learned

Life can be tough on the streets. Although violence is one option in response to bullying, it is not at all the best to resolve conflicts. In contrast to the fear of city streets, play afforded children the experience of freedom.

RIDING BIKES

One sign of growing freedom and independence beyond the city block—bordered by Glenwood Road on the north, Campus Road on the south, East 26th Street on the west, and East 27th Street on the east—was riding a bike. Just south of Campus Road was Brooklyn College, which even included a lily pond as a place to rest and observe carp swimming. Just west of 26th Street was Midwood High School where I attended from 1963 to 1966. Such close proximity to high school meant that during senior year, with a triple-tiered schedule to accommodate all the students, I could attend classes from 7:40 to 11:20 am and then hop back into bed if sleep-deprived from completing late night assignments and before cross-country or track team practice.

Brooklyn College campus, where my mom once worked in the library, had broad, connected walkways without curbs to navigate. They were ideal for biking ventures with relatively few pedestrians to avoid. Beyond bike rides, when red wagons were vehicles of choice, the campus had long, curving, semi-circular ramps for deliveries below the street level. These were ideal for wagon racing, provided we didn't tip over in the process with resulting scrapes, all worn with honor.

On the back end of the campus, railroad tracks were fenced off to prevent our access. Over the years a huge hole under the fence was made. Across the set of four tracks used for freight was an old abandoned train depot that excited imaginative stories of bums living and carousing close by. Such stories led to surveillance teams who cautiously approached the depot to observe those bums. The bums usually turned out to be local teens seeking a place for drinking beer and gawking at pornographic magazines, the remains of which we discovered.

The college provided open grass areas for play if we avoided the ever-marauding campus security. We could easily outrun or navigate an escape with bikes when they stopped our play. In the case of the high-fenced football and baseball fields, we managed to climb those with special care. Those fields provided the added surprise of finding discarded baseballs, tennis balls, and even a practice catcher's mitt used to warm up relief pitchers, which I still possess.

One added benefit was the opportunity to actually view college students in their classes when we, with stealth, toured the classroom buildings. I recall thinking, "It would be fun to go to college someday," upon viewing biology labs where interesting specimens were dissected before our very eyes.

The other game we played was to wrestle on the sidewalks, blocking the coeds' access and requiring them to step over us while wearing skirts. This provided the occasion of wild claims to have seen their underpants, noting the color. Laughter ensued until they soon learned just to walk around us and avoid our antics.

Eventually campus security appeared with shouts directed to us, "You kids get up and out of here! We are going to call your parents once we catch you!" They never did, but their threats quickened our conscience with reminders of Sunday school lessons, "Be careful little eyes what you see. Be careful little eyes what you see. There's a Father up above, and he's looking down in love. So be careful little eyes what you see."

The one bike I acquired through careful saving was a used Schwinn "truck bike" that had heavy wheels and even shock absorbers. It even had a lock in the front of the frame that set the handlebars and front wheel to the left, preventing theft. Bike theft was an ever-present threat on Brooklyn streets. The huge handlebars provided a platform for sitting. They even accommodated my younger brother Ronnie when he wanted a ride.

One fateful day the ride with Ronnie proved to be a big mistake, issuing in regrets that I can still feel in my gut to this day. By best estimate, Ronnie was five and I twelve years old. Our normal practice was to ride one time around the block. Ronnie and I were so comfortable with this opportunity for sibling bonding that he relaxed his legs into the front wheel without my notice. His right ankle was pinned between the wheel and the bike frame. In such a position the wheel spokes managed to sheer several layers of skin off Ronnie's ankle. When I heard his cries and finally realized what was happening, I stopped the bike and slowly set it down.

It required all my strength to pry his ankle from the bike and roll him and my bike around the corner to inform my mom and get Ronnie medical help. At the time, Doctor Friedman had his office just across the street where I immediately carried Ronnie. With my heart in my throat, I awaited the verdict in the small waiting room, which felt like a cage of guilt. Eventually Ronnie, my mom, and Doctor Friedman emerged with a huge ankle bandage attached. I was relieved to hear Doctor Friedman say, "Ronnie will heal, but no more bike-rides for children on the handle bars." His head rub only slightly relieved the heaviness that lingered for days, realizing that I had unintentionally caused harm to my younger brother who was in my charge.

At the end of the summer before senior year in high school I actually rode my heavy Schwinn truck bike all the way from my Brooklyn neighborhood into Manhattan across the Brooklyn Bridge. Then after navigating Manhattan streets with my buddy George Marmorino, we rode to the Staten Island Ferry Terminal at Battery Park. George was riding an English touring bike that had multiple gears, simplifying the hills of Staten Island. We had some rest while riding the ferry in our quest to surprise a girl I had met at summer camp and her friends. She was, to my great disappointment, not at home. We managed to make the arduous return trip home before dark, having ventured daringly across the three boroughs. We never thought of informing the girls by phone prior to our venture.

Lessons Learned

The freedom of spontaneous play launched on bikes and wagons is worth securing for children. Such play requires the safeguards of supervision for the young and advocacy for open and green spaces, especially in urban areas. U. S. society invests much more in streets, highways, and military expenditures than in the education and care of children. Priorities need to be reset and maintained across the generations.

Free play also requires diligence to prevent handlebar and other accidents in this world. Each of us has the potential for both good and harm in relation to our immediate family and anyone we happen to meet. Such responsibility can weigh heavy on those involved in accidents, with the tendency of children and some youth to blame themselves for all that befall themselves and their loved ones. I recall the clear expectation when growing up, "You are supposed to take care of, to look after your younger brother [and sister], so that they won't get hurt." When that did not happen, my natural tendency was to blame myself. The challenge for children, youth, and adults alike is to forgive ourselves in the midst of life's accidents and tragedies. Personally, this aspect of forgiveness is more possible in recognizing that God forgives us in Jesus Christ.

Given the epidemic rise of pornography in U. S. culture affecting children and youth, the Sunday school admonitions and wisdom for character formation are worth repeating in the light of my sidewalk antics. Electronic access to a variety of media intended for adult viewing provides a new challenge today for those who care for children and youth.

BEACH DAYS

Growing up in the Flatbush section of Brooklyn meant we had relatively easy access to the beach. Jacob Riis Park on the Atlantic Ocean in Queens, and currently a part of the National seashore, was just a short ride away on the green bus lines. Riis Park was situated just east of Fort Tilden, which was an active Army fort where my dad was stationed for a brief time before serving in the Pacific arena during World War II. On our bus ride down Flatbush Avenue to Riis Park on the Brooklyn side, we would pass Floyd Bennett Field, which was a National Guard airfield just before the Marine Parkway Bridge. Scouting outings during my boyhood included visits to both the fort and airfield, supporting the option in formative young minds of future military service for our country. But beach days were for less serious thoughts.

Time at the beach provided welcome relief from sweltering summer days and the great adventures of riding the rough surf, digging intricate tunnels and sand castles, burying friends up to their necks, playing in beach playgrounds, buying food at beach concessions, and in adolescence, observing girls in their swim wear. We would board the green bus at the junction of Flatbush and Nostrand Avenues and line up over the subway's metal gratings. The bus fare to the beach was twenty-five cents and a few riders would lose their carefully guarded quarters down the grates.

Here was a treasure trove of coins to access when our finances prevented beach travel. Reaching the treasure required ingenuity and patience. Long strings or lines were needed for this fishing and heavy metal washers were gracefully arranged at the end of the strings. The lowest washer that would secure the quarter needed to be close in diameter to the coin and thickly coated with Vaseline to hold the coin on its long ascent up to street level and into our secure hands. Real skill and patience were required for this job, even more than fishing lost balls from down the sewer grates on the corners of our playground streets. That extraction was accomplished with wire hangers attached to stickball bats and a willingness to lie on the street over the grate. Coins fished up were used to purchase good humor ice cream pops and sandwiches at the beach concessions on hot summer beach days. The other option was to wait until the beach workers brought those treats right to your blanket-side. "Get your ice cold pops here; just fifteen cents!" Our response was, "Over here, over here!" with hands raised to get their attention. Eating those cold treats fast avoided losing any morsel. With sticky hands we ran back to the surf to wash and cool off, often walking on our tip toes across hot sands.

Riis Park offered strong surf with regular high waves and jetties that served to keep the beach from being washed away into the vast Atlantic. The wide expanse of ocean and sky was a welcome alternative to the city landscape and encouraged dreams of travel to far-off places. Our digging of deep holes included the imagined venture of finding China on the other side of the globe. The beach crowd also offered the chance to observe other city dwellers up close and personal. New friends and acquaintances could be made in such close quarters.

At the water fountain and washing trough near the boardwalk children would often gather with their buckets and shovels. One day at the beach with John Reily when we were seven years old, we happened to encounter a friendly African American boy our age also playing there. John carefully whispered in my ear "Don't touch him, because if you do, you'll turn black." I risked the encounter and touched the potential newfound friend and didn't turn black. Back at our blanket I showed John my hands and arms "Look, I didn't change and he was a nice boy."

John wasn't convinced and maintained fears of African Americans that were common in our neighborhood. My mom occasionally voiced such fears that emerged from her days growing up in Philadelphia. This contrasted with her positive relationships with African Americans at our church and later in her Brooklyn College work place. My dad would dismiss negative racial and ethnic slurs and question stereotyping of others with his "Bah, bah!" He did not tolerate what he considered to be nonsense.

One incident that reinforced John's fears was when we worked hard together to sell a whole box of candy bars for the Boys' Club, a bus ride away on Nostrand Avenue near Church Avenue. We had joined together.

On the bus ride back to the club, John had proudly told an older African American boy who was riding with us that we had sold all our bars in one day. I tried to signal John not to boast about our success. Upon getting off the bus, the boy pulled John into a doorway with a knife to his neck demanding all the money.

When we told our story to the Boys' Club director, he was skeptical and required us to march with him directly to the nearby local police station to recount our holdup to a police officer. "We are not lying and didn't spend the money!" was our plea, but we never returned to the club and harbored fears of future encounters with other African American youth in our Brooklyn adventures.

Lessons Learned

Living in close proximity to the beach provided a blessed alternative to hot apartments and city streets. We also opened fire hydrants to cool off, though it was illegal. Eventually the New York City fire department installed sprinklers on some key hydrants to provide alternatives in Brooklyn neighborhoods.

Beaches and other public spaces provided the opportunity for different racial and ethnic groups to interact beyond the common stereotypes perpetuated both in and out of our homes. Both good and bad folk can be found in any group, calling for caution and discernment in daily encounters. My experience across those divides in childhood and youth were overwhelmingly positive, supported by an inclusive neighborhood culture and the values of my extended family and local church. Jesus' teaching about loving our neighbor as ourselves took on immediate relevancy with all the different folk living elbow to elbow in Brooklyn.

HALLOWEEN

My neighborhood, dominated by six-floor apartment buildings, was a bonanza on Halloween. My buddies John Reily and Scott Drake and I devised a scheme to maximize our candy and coin returns. Our scheme required careful planning and time coordination. After all, we did announce "trick *and* (rather than *or*) treat" to all our unsuspecting neighbors.

Right after arriving home from school on Halloween afternoon, we each selected two separate costumes for our venture. One remained laid out on our beds with a mask; the other we wore first without a mask. We kept our bedroom doors closed to maintain pre-adolescent privacy and avoid parents' unwanted inquiries.

We all found old calf-high athletic socks in which we placed long sticks of pastel chalk, preferably red, yellow, or purple. These colors could be seen even on dark hallway walls. We tightly knotted the socks just above the chalk. Before beginning our rounds, we pounded our chalk socks against the sidewalk pavement in front of 2620 Glenwood Road. These socks were good protection from older marauding trick-or-treaters who sought to steal our treats. We discovered another clever use for them.

We first started with our building, just when most folk would be home, working our way down from the top to bottom floors. At each apartment door, we knocked hard shouting out "trick *and* treat." If our treats were really good and once the doors were shut, we quietly marked with chalk the wall above or next to that apartment.

Our rounds continued to the five apartment houses that averaged ten families per floor. After two hours our shopping bags were bursting to the brim, but it was only at half time.

We rushed back to our homes, dumped out bags on our beds, and quickly changed into our second costumes, this time with masks. We drank some water, had a bathroom break, and then re-traced our canvass across the buildings. This time we streamlined the process by only knocking at the marked doors, disguising our voices when needed to avoid detection. We kept our laughter in check between floors with our ingenious deception.

You see, Scott learned from his stories at Hebrew school, John from CCD (Confraternity of Christian Doctrine), and I from Sunday school about Passover. God's faithful marked the doorposts and lintels of their homes. They avoided disaster and received gold, silver, and precious gems from the Egyptians in the process. We, as an improvement, used chalk instead of blood, and received a double portion of Halloween treats.

After bragging to friends about our flawless scheme and overindulging the sweets that year, we returned to normal trick *or* treating next Halloween. We also knew building superintendents did not appreciate their additional cleanup of walls. We somehow avoided adult detection, but not without a sense of guilt over the years for deceiving unsuspecting neighbors.

Lessons Learned

Greed, especially for candy, can motivate creative exploration. At the age of twelve, we did not consider how our deception affected ourselves and others who might not receive a double portion of sweets.

BOOK FROM REDDY

One of my Christmas gifts that survived over the years was from my older neighbor who lived just across the hallway from apartment 4G. The dedication of *Old Testament Stories: Retold for Children* reads the following: "To Bobby from Reddy, December 25, 1956." It has a bright red cover with a simple illustration of

David the young shepherd tenderly holding a lamb in his crook with the lamb's mother ewe walking beside him and baying. This same scene of David appears in full opposite the title page. David is on a hilly path and surrounded by an entire herd of sheep. David appears to be about my age at the time and with dark brown hair just like mine. The work is written by Lillie A. Faris and illustrated by W. Fletcher White. Inside the front cover is another portrayal of David seated and reassuring an ewe by patting her head. He is still holding the lamb in his arms and right next to him on a huge rock is his harp, ready to soothe beast or human in troubled times. This portrayal captures well what I imagine the shepherd who wrote the Twenty-third Psalm looked like. Right above David in the open space of the sky my personal stamp appears in blue ink:

> Robert Pazmiño
> 2620 Glenwood Road
> Brooklyn 10, NY
> Phone Gedney 4–8355.

My stamp secured proof of ownership.

The table of contents lists stories, beginning with Noah and the Ark and ending with "A Queen Who Saved Her People." For each story I read, a checked pencil mark appears on its line. If I read it a second time, the pencil mark is outlined with an orange crayon. Here is a careful accounting of accomplished reading, not unlike the series of perfect attendance pins received at a church service for perfect Sunday school attendance. I faithfully keep an account of the stories that shaped my life.

I wonder why my *Old Testament Stories* does not begin with Adam and Eve, but I recall that in the beginning they were naked in the garden. Retelling requires editing for young eyes. Looking at pictures of naked people is certainly not to be encouraged, especially in a Bible storybook. But childhood curiosity was not squelched with that editorial omission. I did get to see my older sister's body when we took baths together as preschoolers and had an occasional glance of my mom coming out of the shower. Questions about differences in bodies weren't asked, but sung about:

"Bobby and _____ sitting in a tree K-I-S-S-I-N-G. First comes love, then comes marriage, then comes Bobby and _____ pushing a baby carriage." Teasing continued through elementary school until junior high when affections were more serious and potentially volatile.

Reddy was often home bound and my mom always reached out to neighbors meeting unmet needs. She was a deaconess at church. As soon as I was old enough to do food shopping solo, Reddy hired me to do her food shopping, carefully printing out a prepared list. Before heading out with her wheeled shopping cart, Reddy showed me the near-empty containers for each of the items listed with no substitutes allowed. I searched the rows and shelves at the local Bohack Super Market, a one-time city chain, up on Flatbush Avenue. I would ask for help from store clerks if any item could not be found. I did not want to disappoint Reddy when I returned with her weekly food order. She was always delighted when I showed her all the items she requested as I extracted them from the brown paper bags.

Lessons Learned

Caring for neighbors builds a sense of community. Shared stories, especially from the Bible, help provide meaning in our lives and can be passed on.

MARIO AND SEWER BALLS

Every Brooklyn neighborhood had their share of *screwballs* we would try to avoid at all costs on the streets. In the case of Glenwood Road, we had Mario. Mario was an older teenager who scoured the neighborhood in search of rubber balls used for playing stickball. He carried a vintage stickball bat with its handle wrapped in opaque black electrical tape. These bats were often made of sawed down broom handles ideal for recycling in street games.

Mario could hit any ball a mile. He demonstrated his skill to us: "Watch me, watch me hit!" was his frequent plea. He needed an adequate ball supply to entice others to play with him on the back end of the handball court wall that had a strike zone painted on it. The long balls he hit usually landed on or over the roof of P. S. 152, well out of reach for retrieval. We were never sure if he would use his bat on us if we didn't help him in his frantic ball search. Mario rhythmically tapped the bat on the street or sidewalk, giving us adequate warning of his approach while listening to his hand-held portable radio.

Mario typically wore over-sized, long green shorts secured with a dangling thick black belt too long for his narrow waist, a dirty striped polo with obvious holes, and black high-top converse sneakers with white socks that barely covered his grimy ankles. All the pockets of his shorts were stuffed with balls. His close-cropped haircut barely covered his pockmarked scalp, which he would often pick at. I sometimes wondered what had happened in Mario's life that contributed to his frenzied ball search up and down the neighborhood streets, placing fear into the hearts of all he encountered who were requested to help him.

"Hey, you, you, you guys have any balls for me?" Mario blurted out on his approach.

"No, but we lost some down the sewer on the corner" we sheepishly replied.

If that was the truth, we were relieved to send him off. Mario carried with him one or two wire hangers that had been untwined and reshaped. They became long hooks with a circular cup fashioned to tightly fit a rubber ball through the holes in the sewer grating with ease. Mario was a master at sewer ball retrieval. He would lie down over the sewer grate and lower his wire hook into the dark abyss below street level. I wondered, "Does Mario have x-ray vision to see into the sewer abyss just like superman?"

Once a ball was slipped into the wire cup out of the smelly sewer waste, Mario slowly and skillfully raised it through the grating or just near enough to the sewer opening below the curb for grasping with his free hand.

While playing stick or punchball on the city streets, our challenge was to avoid losing our balls down the ever-present sewer openings where retrieval was nearly impossible, except for with Mario's help. Balls that stewed in the sewer were typically discolored on their lower half by the pungent mix. Those well-ripened balls were of particular fascination for Mario. Once secure at street level and dried up by rolling them under foot on the baking sidewalk, those balls delighted him. They were held by Mario close to his nose and lovingly smelled all the way to the playground.

If we lied to Mario about losing our balls in the sewer, then we waited until he positioned himself over the grate.

"Don't let Mario see us leaving," we warned each other in whispers.

Only then we slowly moved off the street and waited out of sight in the lobby of our apartment building, peering out through the stained glass window over the radiator consoles. We stood on the consoles to see out the one missing pane, which provided a good view of the sidewalk. If Mario abandoned his search, he walked by the playground with the stickball court on Bedford Avenue.

If Mario glanced up and saw us departing, he yelled out:

"Hey, you, you guys get back here!" as we ran for our lives.

Thankfully, Mario had a short memory and perhaps avoided us on his next pass through the neighborhood, especially if fascinated with the smell of one of his rare finds. He would maraud the neighborhood streets bouncing each of his sewer balls to discover which had the best bounce in preparation for stickball challenges. To stay on his good side, we would always greet him in passing on the stickball court:

"Hey, Mario!" we shouted with arms lifted and waving in the air.

On a rare occasion, we might even call on him to come to our aid when confronted with threats from out-of-neighborhood bullies who were also marauding on Mario's territory. Stick-wielding Mario was a powerful ally for just such occasions.

"Hey, Mario, these guys want to steal your balls!"

Our call would send them running, upon seeing his wild and bat-wielding approach.

Some folk may be troubled, but may have a niche to fill in this life. The recovery of sewer balls contented Mario and enabled him to play his beloved stickball. This was his rare pleasure. What others avoided at all costs, he was able to use and even play with. He was an ally worth having on Brooklyn streets.

Lessons Learned

Even *screwballs* can be valued for their community contributions. My mom always taught and modeled for us that everyone was to be respected and valued as loved unconditionally by God. Later in life, when she worked at the Brooklyn College Library she befriended a tall, black transgendered co-worker by the name of Francis whom most folk avoided. My dad often prepared lunch for Francis and mom to welcome them. My interest and love for people led to the study of psychology in college, and eventually inspired me to enter ministry and develop a career in theological education.

CANARSIE PIER AND MY PEERS

My dad loved fishing whenever his busy schedule would allow such a luxury. When I went fishing one day with my father at Canarsie Pier in Brooklyn, I had a glimpse of what community can mean.

Canarsie Pier was reached, in our case, by car off of the Belt Parkway that connects the coastline of Brooklyn with New York Harbor, Sheepshead Bay, and the Atlantic Ocean. Others traveled by foot or public transportation to gain access to the pier, an ideal setting for fishing while watching the water and other New Yorkers at play.

People from every racial, ethnic, and cultural group representing New York were fishing together. Women and men, girls and boys were fishing, and a sense of harmony and community existed among those people assembled on a hot, sun-drenched summer day. Everyone shared in the activity and joy of fishing. People shared their fishing bait, their fishing advice, their fishing stories, and even themselves in an amazing way. This was just one small illustration of what Jesus intended for his followers and what God intends for those called into the new reign of Jesus Christ. This new reign also includes a distinctive call to serve others who are neighbors brought together in a common activity or a common cause, like fishing.

Neighborhoods can embrace the possibility of a common good that links folk together across the wide diversity of humanity, like that encountered in Canarsie and many urban centers across the globe.

Rupert Meldenius, a pseudonym for Peter Meiderlin (1582–1651), an irenic Lutheran theologian who taught and died in Augsburg, is attributed with a saying that others attribute to St. Augustine of Hippo: "In essentials unity, in nonessentials liberty, in all things love." Community can be built around essentials. In the case of fishing, essentials included fishing line, bait, the idea or possibility of fish lurking off the pier, and stories shared. Those stories could be identified as nonessentials, but as they were shared became fun and bonding for all the folk assembled. With the liberty to share came the experience of love in all things.

A multicultural and diverse ideal for community, glimpsed at Canarsie Pier, played out for me in relation to my boyhood buddies. Scott Drake, who lived on the third floor of my apartment building, was from a Jewish family, along with Melvin Belsky and Mark Foreman. Scott's dad worked in the Manhattan garment district and he and I both had older sisters—Carol and Laura Lou, respectively. I was introduced to a wealth of Jewish cuisine and humor with Scott and his family. I even visited him when his family moved to Long Island, which became a haven for Brooklyn families moving out of the city in search of a better life and more open spaces. When my own family considered that same move, my older sister and I loudly protested:

"We can't move and leave all of our friends and this neighborhood! I know we will hate it on the Island!"

Our protests and the potentially longer commute for my dad won the day. Even the great low VA loan rates for real estate could not compete with the importance of friends and life in Brooklyn.

Mark Foreman's family introduced me to the reality of persons with disabilities and how they navigated life. Both of Mark's parents were deaf. Their first floor apartment in the neighboring building was equipped with special lights when the doorbell rang, and they had a special phone too. Mark's parents always had a positive attitude about life and its challenges, and Mark was adept at signing with them, which fascinated me. It was evident that despite the odds people confronted in city life, resilience was evident, even in the small things like unheard doorbells.

John Reily was my Irish Catholic friend and he too had an older sister—Beth. Surviving bossy older sisters required an alliance that we nurtured each day, as we sought free spaces outside our apartments for play and mischief. Our mischief came under the surveillance of our superintendent, who came with his family from Yugoslavia. Though his English was limited, he memorized our apartment numbers and shouted them out when he caught us doing unacceptable things or exploring off-limit spaces in the basement or on the roof:

"4G, 3H and 6A, tell parents!"

He followed up on his threats and tried to recount our misdeeds to unsuspecting moms:

"Boys do bad, boys throw water and make mess. No good, no good!"

We tried to convince our moms we were being blamed for anything that went awry by the scrupulous secret police agent from a communist country. That held some weight, until our older sisters chimed in with their untimely eye-witness accounts. This indicated all the more a need for our alliance with efforts to subvert their unwelcome oversight. Sibling rivalries played out across our faith differences with the common cause of boy freedom.

Friendship with Scott meant I attended his bar mitzvah along with that of Melvin and Mark. At one of those events I wore the required yarmulke and prayer shawl. I was so immersed in the prayer service that my entire body swayed in synch with the congregation. My movement managed to gain the attention of the roving rabbi. He tapped my shoulder and said something in Hebrew unintelligible to me. I asked my friend:

"What did he say to me?"

"You learned your prayers well!"

Friendship with John meant I entered for the first time the huge Catholic Church located on Bedford Avenue where he attended. I had been told by my sister not to attend. Because as a Protestant, I was warned, upon entering that church I would die right on the spot.

When at home I reported, "Laura Lou, I didn't die when I went into the Catholic Church today. You lied!"

"You just wait, God is going to punish you and you will die!"

She was right. Eventually I will die, but not from entering a Catholic church. After all, I later learned that my great, great grandfather was actually a Dominican priest in Ecuador and he always went into that kind of church. He even had a household outside the church with his own family.

I learned from Charlie Prado how lessons from church needed to connect with our life on the streets. One late Friday night after our Boy Scouts meeting walking along Amersfort Place, we encountered Teddy drunk, lying between two parked cars, and stabbed in his leg. Teddy was one of the local teens who had run-ins with the police for breaking into stores. I was fearful of the gang violence that took its toll with neighborhood stabbings and suggested we call the police for the help Teddy needed, leaving him there. Charlie rightfully insisted:

"We need to carry Teddy back to the church, administer first aid and call for Pastor Fred Gibson to assist us."

We followed Charlie's lead and Teddy was taken by ambulance with Pastor Fred to the hospital. The lessons of the Good

Samaritan were brought home in caring for Teddy and overcoming my fears of also being stabbed if Teddy's assailants reappeared.

Jack Home was my one Chinese friend who was member of both the Boy Scouts and Kenilworth Baptist Church. Jack's family owned Home's Laundry on Flatbush Avenue where my dad's business shirts were weekly cleaned and pressed. My job was to pick them up, all nicely wrapped and tied in brown paper. Jack patiently taught me one Christmas season how to wrap gifts using the skills learned at his family's business. When calling for Jack to play ball we loved to enter the laundry and chime in unison, smiling:

"Jack home?"

To my surprise Jack followed me to Bucknell University the year after I entered college. I imagine Pastor Fred encouraged him to consider a Baptist-related school just as he did with me.

Lessons Learned

Crossing forbidden borders involves risk, but shared human activities like fishing and worshipping can invite learning and address fears long held. My Brooklyn neighborhood provided a relatively safe setting for my border crossing early in life. It also nurtured a sense of the human community that transcends all the divisions we manage to construct in dealing with difference, especially in the United States with all of its diversity, which threatens some folk.

REFLECTIONS ON COMMUNITY

My neighborhood provided the matrix in which my early life unfolded. It was an interfaith, multicultural, and multiracial setting that shaped my view of the world. Difference among people, for the most part, was not viewed as a deficiency. This stood in contrast with the dominant ethos of the United States. Difference was a curiosity and invited both learning and discovery. Difference was potentially a gift, if a safe space was secured for all persons to equally participate finding a common ground across all measures of variety.

The community supported and supplemented families and provided for some alternatives to what familial expectations might dictate. While celebrating one's identity in the local community, receptivity varied depending upon one's class and faith associations. Boundaries were clear in the case of one's love interests and who was acceptable to date or marry. Examples of those who successfully crossed such borders were not apparent as public role models, except for the case of the Brooklyn Dodgers. My father's Ecuadorean roots were named an issue only years later by an uncle who lived in a more racially and ethnically divided Philadelphia neighborhood. When I was visiting his family with Wanda, my Puerto Rican wife, my uncle commented:

"Those Puerto Ricans are awful people and so different from your dad's Spanish roots!"

Wanda graciously disclosed later in our discussion: "My mom is in Puerto Rico checking on her home there, where she is from."

No further comments about Puerto Ricans were shared during our visit. But on some rare occasions, my mother would make racial comments if reports of violence by African Americans were highlighted in news reports. Her comments contrasted with her usual behaviors, and my sister and I during our teens years pointed out her glaring inconsistencies. Negative behaviors my siblings and I demonstrated were attributed—by my mother—to our father's family, in contrast with hers. Her comments resulted in our laughter because we knew better from stories of her actual experiences growing up and being both excluded and abused as later disclosed. Her move to New York City and our Flatbush neighborhood stretched her to embrace a more inclusive community as we lived that reality out with neighbors daily.

For me, Brooklyn was a setting where cultures collide and persons navigate their emergence. Brooklyn, known as the borough of churches, helped form me as a religious professional in the post-World War Two northeast. One colleague at a professional conference identified me as "part of the eastern establishment" in theological education. How did that happen for a bi-cultural Hispanic North American who journeyed with a diverse host of folk growing up during the 50s and 60s in New York? Over the past thirty years I have jokingly identified myself as a missionary from Brooklyn to New England, teaching and forming current and future spiritual leaders to celebrate their roots and embrace their religious callings.

2

Family

BECAUSE CELIBACY DIDN'T WORK, I'M HERE

My great-great grandfather, Mariano Auz, served as a Dominican priest in Quito, Ecuador during the nineteenth century. Celibacy was not typically observed that far from Rome in colonial Ecuador and, as reported by our family chronicler first cousin Joseph Dudley, it was a common practice for Catholic priests to have a household separate from their parish work. Indeed, my great grandfather Mariano had a common law marriage with Dolorés López, also from Quito. They had five sons together including Felicísimo López (1847–1917), who was my great grandfather and brought his own extended family to New York City in 1900. He had a long-standing marriage and five sons, assuring stability for our own well-established family roots despite stated ecclesial policies.

Felicísimo was a physician and very active in the progressive politics of his time, which sought radical change from conservative and Catholic political powers that dominated all aspects of Ecuadorean life. He served as the Minister of the Interior, overseeing aspects of the educational system under the Alfaro presidency, which brought about liberal reforms. As generational conflicts and fragmentation go, Felicísimo popularized his political views in the press, criticizing church dominance closely aligned with conservative interests. As a result of his public stances and scathing critique of German clerics in the Ecuadorean hierarchy, he was excommunicated from the Catholic Church. Excommunication resulted in the ostracism of our family from ecclesial, social, and cultural circles, leading Felicísimo to apply for diplomatic service in search of a better life.

In 1900 he arrived in New York City with diplomatic papers, bypassing Ellis Island where most immigrants landed. He was appointed the Consul General for Ecuadorean citizens and traveled with his wife Francisca Romero (1850–1940), and my grandparents, Víctor Manuel Pazmiño (1871–1944) and Lelia López (1877–1962). Víctor and Lelia brought along with them their first-born son, my uncle Víctor Estenio Pazmiño (1899–1970). Felicísimo and family eventually settled in Brooklyn, purchasing a home on Glenwood Road that was, at that time, in open fields converted from farm lands.

Notably, Felicísimo was the subject of an essay I wrote on the theme "pioneers in my family" for an English course with Mrs. Haas during my junior year in high school, which is reproduced here. I received a grade of 95 percent (out of a possible 100), the teacher commenting: "What a fine story! You should write his biography someday":

"Felicísimo López, my great grandfather, was a pioneer and made a great contribution to his country. He was born in Guayaquil, Ecuador in 1847. Felicísimo studied medicine and became a doctor in order to serve his people. After practicing medicine for a time he decided to enter politics and became a member and leader of the Liberal Party. During the 1880s and 1890s Ecuador was in the hands of dictatorship with no education for all and few public improvements. The common people were subjected to great hardship and abuses. Land and wealth was concentrated in a selective group of government and church officials. The land was kept unproductive and the people led a harsh life. Discontent rose against the government, led by Liberal leaders in order to relieve these conditions. Felicísimo, being influential in the movement, was exiled to Lima, Peru and the conservative government remained in power.

The Catholic Church owned a majority of the land holdings and supported the actions of the conservative government. Catholic priests from Germany and Spain controlled the actions of the church. Felicísimo wrote pamphlets protesting the church's activities and because of this he was excommunicated.

Finally in 1896 the dictatorship was overthrown and Dr. López returned to his country. The Liberal party gained control of the government and Felicísimo was elected to the Ecuadorean Congress. He was refused his seat in Congress by conservative factions, but through the protest of his constituents he was allowed to assume his position. President Alfaro, then the Liberal President of Ecuador, was the personal friend of Felicísimo, who was chosen to be the Minister of the Interior in the Cabinet and also to serve as an ambassador to Venezuela. Strong in his convictions for equal opportunity for the common man, he was instrumental in beginning the first public school system of Ecuador. He also encouraged the establishment of a greatly needed road system connecting Quito, Ecuador, the capital, and Guayaquil, the main seaport.

Felicísimo maintained a newspaper in Guayaquil and believed in the freedom of press. He compiled throughout his life a collection of short essays, expressing his ideas and thoughts on government, religion, and the workings of his country. These essays were published as a book entitled *Virutas*, literally meaning wood shavings or cuttings. He came to New York City in 1900 to serve as Consul General from Ecuador and later decided to remain in the United States.

Felicísimo died in 1917, glad to have served his people and country. Dr. López died a pioneer and a man of great courage. Today, there is a memorial, erected in front of a high school in Ecuador, to honor his service."

While I have not written Felicísimo's biography as Mrs. Haas suggested, my son David, in his undergraduate honors thesis for

Wesleyan University traced the liberal reforms of Ecuador that represented a model for revolutionary change in Latin America. Felicísimo was an advocate for and implementer of those changes in his political work.

On a visit to Ecuador in 1989, when I visited Catholic University, I shared about Felicisimo, and the comment of one knowledgeable secretary was "*muy rojo*" to describe him. *Muy rojo* means "very red" and referred to the fact that my great grandfather's political ideology was socially democratic, which from a conservative Catholic perspective is associated with communism. My reading of his work in Spanish, *Virutas*, does not comport with that assessment, but I understand this association with the liberal democratic changes that worked for the separation of church and state in Ecuador. That separation allowed for freedom of religion, divorce, and general secular education outside of the church's explicit teaching and its alliance with conservative political factions. Those changes would not be supported or read with appreciation at Ecuador's Catholic University.

Lessons Learned

History will be viewed differently from distinct vantage points. Family traditions and genes have an influence on an individual's choice related to one's values and commitments. In my case, that includes the choice of my lifework in education and my association with American Baptists. American Baptists historically have advocated for the separation of church and state and the soul liberty of each person in embracing their religious convictions.

ABUSE AND LOSS

Laura Ruth Roney (1920–2007), my mom, was born in Pennsylvania of Dutch and German heritage (and possibly French as well). Her German heritage was known as Pennsylvania Dutch. Such a lineage also could refer to "Double Dutch" in Brooklyn, given the sidewalk jump rope game played by children and youth. This game is played with two jump ropes turned in tandem but rotating in opposite directions, requiring a unique combination of jumping and coordination to successfully maintain balance. In her own life, my mom sought balance by leaving Pennsylvania and moving to New York City when she was eighteen to find work and a new beginning.

My mom was the only child born of her parents' second marriages. Both of their first spouses had died, and I recall stories of hardships encountered in her blended family with her health issues requiring long hospitalizations for ear surgery. Through it all, mom was a survivor that included weathering the death of both her parents when she was a teenager. Their death necessitated her move to the home of one of her married older half-brothers, where I suspect abuse occurred.

Her escape to the big city promised a new start; she was employed as a dental assistant in Brooklyn. While working, mom pursued her love for dancing on weekends, including occasional trips to Catskill mountain lodges. On one of those weekends she met Albert Pazmiño, who also loved to dance and socialize. In proximity to a global city like New York, it was possible for an Ecuadorean-American young man to meet a Double Dutch young woman. Marriage followed, but also World War II, which brought my dad to serve in the U. S. Army in the Pacific arena.

During the war my dad served as a technical sergeant, overseeing all the records of his division as they traveled to various islands. Prior to the war, my dad worked as a court stenographer and his office skills found a niche in his military service. I recall stories of what my dad cooked with his army buddies more than any combat tales. The one exception was his explanation for the dimple in his chin, claiming a war wound. My dad explained, "I happened to be stationed at the end of the war in Hiroshima. Our unit was in disarray and one day when the atomic bomb hit I was looking up in the sky. The bomb hit my chin leaving me this big dimple!"

A Boy Grows in Brooklyn

Following the war my parents started their family with twins, a boy and a girl, born December 1946. Laura Lou survived that birth, but not Albert Jr., who lived for only an hour. I often wondered about the older brother I never knew, which led me to write the following letter to him. One of my former students, Professor Tina Wray, has written about grieving the loss of siblings and has an online ministry in this area. She would commend my effort to name this loss not shared in print until now:

Dear Albert,

I have always wanted to meet you, but you died before I was born. I always wanted an older brother to look up to and teach me. Being a fraternal twin to our sister Laura Lou, I imagine you may have been in some important ways both like her and different. She survived your shared birth and we still talk and laugh, sharing by phone what growing up in Brooklyn was like.

I understand that you only lived on this earth for a short time and I wonder what life would have been like together growing up in the 50s and 60s in our Flatbush neighborhood.

In some ways, I think the hopes our mom and dad had for you by naming you Albert, after dad, were passed along to me when I was born a year and a half later. Mom told me that, like Hannah from the Old Testament who prayed for Samuel's birth, she dedicated her next-born son to God's service. For Brooklyn Catholic families that meant having a child become a priest or nun, or for Protestants, a minister. Mom's prayer was fulfilled when I was ordained in Christian ministry and taught at theological institutions for the past thirty years.

I was also expected to succeed at school and to achieve something in my life that was worthy of our family name. I hope I leave a lasting legacy through published works that someday may include this letter to you.

I imagine you would have been something like our cousin Joseph, who was five years older than you, or cousin Kenneth, who was fifteen years older. I looked up to them while growing up. They both left Brooklyn and a legacy that was passed on in family chronicles and architectural designs found in many public places. They realized the dream our great grandfather Felicísimo López had when he came to the United States from Ecuador to find a new life for our family. He hoped for educational opportunities in an open society. His thoughts are recorded in his journal, written in 1900 when he arrived in New York City with diplomatic papers as the Counsel General for Ecuadorean citizens.

I missed playing ball with you and going to the beach. I missed receiving the wisdom you would have gained from surviving the hard knocks of our Flatbush neighborhood.

You would have loved the extended family gatherings we still have and getting to know all the unique neighbors in our apartment building. There is a special legacy our parents passed along to us, and you would have a part in all that we experienced together into our adult lives.

I wish you could meet my wife Wanda, whom everyone loves, and our children and grandchildren. They too would love you as I do. I look forward to meeting you on the other side of death, spending time together in the eternity promised by my faith. I have sought in my life to be the big brother to others that I imagine you would have been for me.

Your loving brother,
Bobby

Lessons Learned

Abuse and loss need to be named to avoid continued harm and to allow for healing and the mending of lives. Humor provides one outlet for addressing tragedy, but cannot deny the real horrors of war. Life often involves a balancing game of joy and sorrow shared in community with others. I recall a popular proverb learned in childhood: "A joy shared is twice the joy and a sorrow shared is half the sorrow."

My mom survived experiences that would have crushed others. She maintained a positive outlook on life through it all. Her perspective is reflected in her favorite number thirteen, which most folk associated with bad luck. Mom was born on August 13, married on the December 13, died on June 13 and is buried in section thirteen of Calvert Memorial Cemetery next to her beloved husband. Her great grandson Eli Theodore Pazmiño was born on August 13, 2009 two years after her death. The reversal of fortunes in life calls us to resilience and hope.

NANA AND SHOPPING

My grandmother Lelia, known to us as Nana, was the only grandparent I ever knew growing up. All the others passed away before I was born, but who were introduced to me via photos shared at family gatherings. Nana was thus my only visible link to life in Ecuador, apart from occasional visits to Brooklyn from extended family who shared fascinating accounts of life in South America. Their accounts served as a reminder that the United States is not the only "America," with a host of other countries in North, Central, and South Americas.

Nana was short in stature with thinning gray hair that was wrapped in a bun and held in place with black barrettes. She always wore a black hat, along with black or dark clothing, and a cardigan that was carefully buttoned to keep warm on cold days. All of her black clothing and accessories complemented her stern demeanor. This somber mood appeared as her way of grieving the loss of her long-deceased husband, her dislocation in Brooklyn from her beloved Ecuador, and her diminished standard of living compared to her previous upper-class life. Her home was slowly deteriorating due to a lack of funds for necessary repairs with no hope of future changes in income.

Nana also had a host of small bumps and growths that grew on her aging face that are now appearing on mine. My observant grandson, Eli, caringly inquires about these facial features thinking they are like his bumps and cuts:

"Are they better, grandpa?"

I reply, "Yes, and how are yours?"

In so doing, Eli shares his recent wounds and their state of recovery.

My dad and I weekly accompanied Nana, my grandmother, for her food shopping at the local A & P store located on Flatbush Avenue. Nana, who lived with my uncle Victor, her son, in a large private home on Glenwood, did not own a car, so needed our assistance to manage her weekly shopping trips. Nana wrote her shopping list on a small slip of paper that was secured in the front compartment of her hefty black leather handbag.

Nana scrupulously checked the prices of every item on her list, placed the ones that met her standards in the shopping cart I would push for her. For every item she selected, Nana would have me reach in the back of each pile on the shelf to extract the most recent additions. This was due to the grocers' anticipations that usually shoppers would quickly select the readily accessible select items in the front of the stack, enabling them to maintain their inventory and avoid outdated discards. Nana knew their tactic and searched out the newest items carefully placed out of reach for most shoppers, especially those of advanced age like her. Nana was not to be fooled as a consumer. Thus, my assigned task as the agile grandson was to dig deep for the precious new products.

Grocers were also in the habit of placing damaged items towards the front with the hope of avoiding shoppers' careful scrutiny. Again, Nana was not to be deceived and checked even the out-of-reach item for any signs of damage. She did not speak much English and preferred her native Spanish, but she managed to give me facial expressions and nods to indicate whether an item was acceptable enough to be placed in her select cart. Even when in acceptable condition, the item's price was checked and compared with her memory of the prices of past weeks to ensure she was not being overcharged. If a price increase was unacceptable I would hear "tiss, tiss," and Nana's Spanish commentary to my dad or Uncle Victor. Their expected response was "Sí, sí," ("yes, yes") confirming her displeasure by shaking their heads in agreement.

It was challenging for me to wait patiently during Nana's grocery item inspection. I could have accumulated her items in a quarter of the time. If the item was damaged or too costly, my job was to return it to the appropriate shelf and pile. However, I often opted to place the item in front rather than the inaccessible back to save time. On some occasions, a store manager or conscientious clerk would spy on my stacking maneuvers to ensure I was not upsetting their system or shelf arrangements; but, Nana's penetrating stare would quickly discourage any planned intervention on their part.

After assembling her weekly groceries, the check-out process would begin. During this time, Nana would position herself ever so close to the cashier to confirm the price being charged for each item. One final check was required once we finally arrived back at Nana's kitchen table. All grocery items, after being removed from the paper bags, were carefully assembled to confirm their prices against the printed receipt. Any discrepancies required a return trip to the A & P where the store manager was called upon to immediately rectify the overcharge. Consequently, until her item review in the kitchen was finished, Nana kept her hat and coat on. Only when all was acceptable with the prices charged would Nana then remove her outer garments and return to her rocking chair, positioned at the large front parlor window of her dreary and often cold house. The rising price of coal required a rationing of the coal deliveries sent down the chute and stored in the room adjacent to the furnace in her dingy basement. From her window perch she was able to scrutinize all of the neighborhood happenings.

Despite her familial ties to the community, Nana refused to pursue United States citizenship. Upon their arrival in 1900, she and her family—which included her parents, my grandfather, and Uncle Victor—received diplomatic standing, so there was little need back then. Her first love was also her native Ecuador, where she always hoped to return to live one day. This never happened. While she managed a brooding existence in Brooklyn at a social level far below that of her earlier life, she would never be cheated in her grocery shopping. When I visited her beloved Quito in 1989, I finally appreciated what she so desperately missed: the beauty of a city surrounded by mountains and eternal Spring weather nurture longterm attachment.

Nana passed away on December 29, 1962, when I was fourteen years old, after suffering a massive stroke in her own home just after Christmas. We received a desperate phone call that night from my uncle. Due to the cost of hospital care, she was first brought to our small two-bedroom apartment, carried by my dad and Uncle Victor in a wooden kitchen chair. My mom and dad were deacons of our church and known for hosting and caring for others in need. However, it soon became apparent that her condition was serious and required hospitalization no matter what the cost.

Not knowing what would happen to Nana, I was given the task of babysitting that night for our neighbor Louise Ritz at her nearby apartment building. She and John had an event to attend and I was the only sitter available. Off I went without knowing how things would turn out with Nana. My mom assured me by saying:

"Bobby, there is nothing you can help with by staying. Go ahead to Louise's home as you promised."

Louise was our church choir director. One of our family summer vacations included a visit to her family's home in Wilkes-Barre, Pennsylvania. Sharing family crises was what we did at church. So, as soon I arrived at her front door, I shared the news:

"My Nana has been brought to our apartment, but needs to go to the hospital. My dad has already called for the ambulance."

She replied: "Thank you for coming and we will be praying for her and your family while we are out tonight."

"Have a good time," were my parting and questioning words as I locked their front door.

I thought to myself, "How can someone wish a good time for others when going through a crisis? Didn't I care for my grandmother who is probably dying tonight? Shouldn't I be with my family instead of making money babysitting? What is it like to die? Nana is old and unhappy. Isn't it better for her to die, even if she doesn't go to church or believe in God?"

Despite the perplexing questions, I managed to put the children to bed. It soon got late and I began to fall asleep in a comfortable, overstuffed plaid armchair while the television hummed at a low volume. At least the children didn't wake up, so my fleeting dreams were undisturbed. In them, I saw Nana reunited with her husband and standing outside a home like one I had seen in photos of Ecuador. She seemed to be laughing and smiling, which was so unlike her, while surrounded by a host of family, including her sister Eloisa and her beloved niece Enid, all enjoying a meal outdoors. Then something went wrong and a loud crash was heard by all.

As it turned out, the apartment door was being unlocked at the same time that the phone was loudly ringing. Louise rushed in while I was too dazed to answer the phone, so as not to wake the children. After hanging up, she told me: "Your mom just called to say that your grandmother died in the hospital. I am so sorry. Come and get a hug."

Louise smelled of lavender perfume and her embrace assured me of the care that those from the church provided in times of loss. Then she thanked me for coming and instructed her husband, "John, please pay Bobby so that he can get home. It is late."

It all seemed as surreal as the cold December night air chilled my whole body on the short walk back home down Cortelyou Road and across to Glenwood. Then it hit me. "Now, I have no grandparents. Death is weird and leaves me empty inside. I wonder how dad is doing now that his mom is dead. He really took care of her all these years."

Hugs welcomed me at home after what seemed like a long elevator ride to the fourth floor and to my apartment 4G.

"What a strange mix of feelings death brings!" I thought.

I dropped into bed, unsettling dreams accompanying my jumbled sleep.

Lessons Learned

Death is an unwelcome visitor, even for the old and sad. Families experience crisis and disorientation in times of loss. Hugs and the presence of others help navigate the passage that ends life on earth, yet life continues on for the living with the commitments one makes, like babysitting for others. The rituals and quirks of Nana's shopping are eclipsed by the time shared in helping each other as a family.

REAL MEN COOK

From my earliest memories, I recall my dad cooking on weekends, my mom handling the task during the week. My dad's process-serving business required him to ride the Interborough Rapid Transit (IRT) subway train on weekdays from the very last stop on the Flatbush line to his office in lower Manhattan. So weekends provided an occasion for him to use his hands and whip up an extensive variety of meals.

My dad's Ecuadorean culture relishes a fiesta initiated by a full weekend breakfast table. Our weekend feast would typically begin with a sumptuous breakfast. My favorite was generously buttered cinnamon raisin toast, but these meals also included homefried potatoes, scrambled eggs, and fried meat. The meat could include bacon, ham, pork sausage, scrapple, and even exotic lamb kidneys sliced and seasoned to perfection. On other days fruit pancakes (of the blueberry, apple, or peach variety) or waffles were featured. Hot and cold cereal was reserved for weekdays, when we would rush to school a few blocks down on Glenwood. However, my mom's Saturday breakfast request included the addition of cottage cheese to the fruit pancakes and drenched in maple syrup. The breads served included hot bagels distinctly made in Brooklyn bakeries with my dad's choice being bialys covered in cream cheese, jams, and marmalades—his favorite was orange marmalade. Plenty of orange juice was also a must, with my mom's addition of cranberry juice, to create my favorite pink juice concoction. Sunday morning breakfasts were less sumptuous with the need to attend both Sunday school and church, which we did together as a family.

Lunch menus included sandwiches of fresh cold cuts on soft deli rolls with layers of lettuce, tomatoes and pickles, and topped with mayonnaise or mustard depending upon the meat selected, and on the side, macaroni or potato salad, with dill or sweet pickles and some kind of chip to match the day's flavorings. My favorite drink was Hawaiian Fruit Punch, which I loved to open using the pointed end of a bottle opener, so I could hear a pop in the process. This was served in a brightly colored aluminum glass filled to the brim with ice cubes and cold to the touch. Mom was careful to always instruct me: "Serve everyone first before your second glass of punch!"

Afternoon playtime was only interrupted with the call to Saturday night dinner, which, in case we were outside, was signaled with my dad's piercing and distinctive whistle or my mom's call.

My dinnertime favorite was breaded steak, homemade French fries, and fresh spinach cooked to perfection and dosed in butter. Cholesterol counting was not the order of the day back then and dinner was often proceeded with *chicharones*, which is fried beef fat, salted and served in a fresh blanket of bread. This was a food lover's heaven.

Food shopping was an integral part of our weekend, and I would accompany my dad either early in the morning or right after our meal. Cleanup was left for my mom and older sister in our household division of labor. Our shopping included stops at a large supermarket, a fruit and vegetable stand, the butcher, a delicatessen, and the bakery. Comparative shopping was always the order of the day, with my dad selecting the freshest items at the lowest cost to complement his creative weekend menus. In today's parlance, he was a "foodie." This family tradition has been passed on to my siblings and me and now resides most deeply in my son, David, who is a culinary professor at Newbury College in Brookline, Massachusetts. He previously worked at *Cooks Illustrated* and still does some special projects and teaching online for them.

My favorite foods growing up and still today are fruits of every kind. I can still hear household inquiries, "Who ate all those delicious ripe plums and grapes? Bobby you need to leave some of those for others!" Over time I learned the importance of sharing and celebrating the enjoyment of others with soul-satisfying food. And I will never forget hearing the sexist observation: "The world's best chefs are men!"

Lessons Learned

Shared sumptuous meals serve to sustain the life of families and to welcome strangers and friends at the table. Years later when I worked with emotionally disturbed children, the most therapeutic times occurred when we prepared and shared meals together. Many of the children did not have this experience in their families of origin. The quality of dialogue and sharing deepened after meals. The shared family table blessed my childhood and youth as it welcomed others.

SUMMER PICNICS

Summers brought with them long-anticipated picnics with extended family, our church family, and friends. Indeed, picnics included all those having any possible connection to our family. The elaborate ritual of packing up the food and the play and swim gear, and the challenge of fitting everyone in over-packed cars without undue upsets served to build the anticipation for our much-needed escapes from city living. The destinations varied and included Valley Stream State Park on Long Island, Anthony Wayne State Park off the Taconic Parkway, and even close by Manhattan Beach that had grills for cooking, which were not available at our preferred Jacob Riis Park, located just over the bridge from Brooklyn to Queens.

We always aimed to leave by 7:00 am in order to reserve the best spot for the day. I recall one of the sayings learned at school and echoed at home, "The early bird catches the worm." This provided a corrective for any morning grumpiness on what was typically a sleep-in day for my older sister. In contrast, I was, and continue to be, a morning person.

Saturday picnics began with breakfast after the charcoals first began burning in the heavy-duty iron grills. After thoroughly dousing the Kingsford charcoal briquettes with lighter fluid, my dad would use his cigarette lighter to start a dry twig or a tightly wrapped strip rolled from one of the paper grocery bags. We used the bags to carry all the bakery goods, snacks, paper plates, cups, and utensils, which required care. Sticking out over the top of the bags were the two adjustable long fork skewers just right for cooking individual hotdog cooking or browning marshmallows at the end of the day. Hopefully, the forked ends were wrapped in aluminum foil to avoid skin or eye poking. Cleaning the skewers was often my job at day's end, and was facilitated by a Brillo steel wool pad after the gluey marshmallow remains were vigorously removed with paper towels or other strips from our multi-purpose paper grocery bags (also used to cover school textbooks).

Breakfast started off with home fries flavored with cut on-ions, salt, pepper and paprika and browned on all sides in one frying pan.

"Dad, breakfast ready yet?"

"Hold your horses! Coming soon!"

A second large pan held mounds of scrambled eggs cooked to perfection, having been whipped up prior to frying with milk. The third pan included either bacon or thick-cut ham. With the bacon choice cooked, the remaining fat provided the additional option of whole fried eggs that bubbled on top with gentle splashing of the fat. It was a fantastic sight to see those steaming pans transferred from the grill onto the heavy wood blackened tables without hot plates. My dad's culinary skills were carefully observed by me and my siblings and replicated in later years.

Rye or pumpernickel bread, sliced fresh from Lord's Bakery or an assortment of Brooklyn-baked bagels, welcomed us to the sumptuous picnic table. On occasion, my dad brought prune

Danish, my favorite, which was cut up into pieces for sharing. Each of us asked "Dad, did you get our favorite?" It was always a test to see if he remembered. He always did.

Full glasses of orange juice or coffee with cream (the adult drink) satisfied our thirst and helped wash down the first of three meals and the numerous pickings in between meal times. Along with the soul-satisfying hot meals, I loved the mounds of fruit, which included my favorites: plums and grapes still cool from the red plaid cold chest at one end of the joined picnic tables to accommodate the day-long feast. All aspects of weekend picnics were carefully orchestrated by my dad and mom and facilitated by famished assistants ready to volunteer.

Right after breakfast and cleanup, cries quickly went up:

"Who wants to play catch or Frisbee?"

"What about badminton or volley ball?"

"Who is ready for the pool/lake/beach [depending on the park]?"

Picnics days included both feasting and playing. In the case of a church outing, the numbers were sufficient to stake out a game of intergenerational softball for anyone interested, no matter the age or sex of the picnicker.

"Who are the captains? Let's begin to choose sides for the game!" I urged everyone.

If swimming was an option, the moms present could be heard, "You all must wait at least an hour before you swim to avoid getting cramps in the water! That is the rule."

"Please, mom, I'll be OK to go early."

"No, go play ball first! No exceptions!"

"Alright, alright," was our reluctant but obedient reply.

When the morning games were over and our stomachs famished once again, we somehow managed to find our way back to the continuing feast. To assure our return trip, I would periodically glance backward to orient myself after we first set off early in the day. Some of my scout training was thus put into practice on the picnic front.

Lunch included even more food choices for the discerning palates. The deli provided us with many choices, including German natural-skin hotdogs doused in pickle relish, Guldens Mustard, Heinz Ketchup, or all three on a lightly toasted bun, and hamburgers with Lipton's Onion Soup dry mix or without, topped with thinly sliced fresh onions and/or juicy red beef tomatoes. These choices were important to honor the wide variety of tastes. Besides the hotdogs, I also loved the grilled kielbasa strips coated in mustard and wedged between the seeded Jewish rye bread. I would often dab the uncoated side of kielbasa with butter even before it was used for the corn on the cob on the dinner menu. Ruffle potato chips or thin pretzels added the perfect crunch to our already over-loaded plates. As with weekend meals at home, my favorite lunch drink was Hawaiian Punch carefully mixed with any orange juice left over from breakfast. Mixology was an interest from my early years in the Pazmiño family of "foodies."

After lunch mom's call went forth:

"It is quiet time for card or board games!"

Beach blankets were readily available for those who wanted to sunbathe on nearby grass meadows. Afternoon activities included swimming or rowing, if available, and if not, games involving balls of all sorts. My favorite was softball, which included as many folks as possible. I advocated either for a repeat of the morning lineups if my team did well, or a change if the score was too lopsided, discouraging competition. I often volunteered:

"I'll change teams if that helps out. I can play any position we need to get started." I was a good ball player, fast on the bases and always taking chances in order to get a run. My passion was just to play and have as much fun as I could in the process. Winning was naturally an interest, but not at the cost of a positive group experience with opportunities to laugh at each others' antics and recount all of the memorable plays on the car ride home. My family was privileged to always own a car, enabling us to escape the city for just a day or week-long vacations upstate or even out of state.

Dinner meals included marinated grilled chicken and flank steak thinly cut on an angle and dripping in its juices, juices just right for dipping with bread. If not already devoured, my mom's homemade German-style potato salad was served along with corn on the cob. Ripe tomatoes and olives added flavor and flare to our feast. Dessert was often comprised of toasted marshmallows, smores, my favorite Italian cookies from Lord's Bakery, or rugelach pastries—that is, if any were left from breakfast. Fresh fruit was also served with the choice of plums, cherries, grapes, peaches, and watermelon. These last items were my favorites.

In the process of the day, my mom had usually befriended an adjoining group by sharing introductions, stories, and food to celebrate our common experiences. The wide variety of cultural and ethnic groups who gathered at New York metropolitan area parks provided ventures in regular border-crossing, modeled for us by practicing hospitality across divides.

"Come here, Bobby. I want you to meet Mrs. Johnson and her son Carl," Mom shared.

"Nice to meet you, Mrs. Johnson. Hey, Carl, you want to play ball?"

Part of my mom's legacy was unconditional love demonstrated for anyone who counter-balanced and contrasted her experiences of abuse and rejection in her family growing up. Our extended and church families provided a marked contrast from the rejection of her own family, especially when she came to New York and married a Hispanic man.

Just as we were one of the first groups to arrive in the morning, our feasted and full caravan was one the last to leave the picnic site. We cherished time away from stuffy summer apartments and sidewalks that radiated heat long into the night. We all returned to our space-limited Brooklyn apartment well fed and exhausted from our picnics, but thoroughly refreshed in spirit and soul from time shared together. Baths and showers followed. Everyone helped carry the remains of the day from the car, up the elevator, and to their appointed storage, ready for our next adventure after a thorough cleaning.

Lessons Learned

Feasting and playing with family who also welcomes strangers and new acquaintances serves to build the human community and sustain social life. Jesus had the right idea when he cooked breakfast for his disciples after they shared in the dramatic experiences of his crucifixion and resurrection. City life could also leave folks reeling and in need of a respite. Thus, recreation is crucial for renewal before the return to daily routines and life's demands.

REFLECTIONS ON FAMILY

Functional families provide the essential building blocks of life for children. Having worked professionally with emotionally disturbed children for five years in a psychiatric setting, I know that some families are dysfunctional.

In my case, the modeling and support I received from my immediate and extended family were essential in launching me from boyhood to adult life. Though challenged economically through the lean years of my father's business, we managed to celebrate all that life had to offer in Brooklyn. More than surviving the urban locale, as children we were encouraged to thrive to the best of our abilities with the help and support of our church family and our sustaining faith in God.

In the case of dysfunctional families in our neighborhood, the children sought out alternative role models to envision what might be possible for their futures. But, even with functional families, other adults apart from the celebrities paraded in the media of television, radio, and newspapers supported our journey to adulthood. In my own experience, the local pastors of Kenilworth Baptist Church and the public school teachers who loved to see others think and learn, directly shaped my life's passions.

The Christian commitments of my immediate family also nurtured a liberating perspective. My family taught me by example that I could be adopted into God's family through my faith in Jesus Christ. This extraordinary invitation was extended to all persons regardless of the dynamics of one's family of origin. My parents also modeled aspects of what I learned about other followers of Jesus.

My dad was like a modern-day Andrew who is described in Scripture as one who was always bringing others to Jesus (John 1:4–42; 6:5–9; 12:20–22). Even before he made a faith commitment when I was seven years old, my dad would always pick up church members who needed a ride on Sunday mornings. After his hand healed following from an accident while fixing a flat tire, which was viewed as miraculous, he attended church, eventually becoming a faithful deacon throughout the rest of his life. I spent many hours working alongside my dad at church, where what we valued as an immediate family was shared with all who attended.

My mom was like Dorcas, also known as Tabitha in Scripture (Acts 9:36–42). Dorcas was a disciple known for her good works, who shared the garments she made with many others. My mom readily shared herself through her teaching, choir singing, and gracious hospitality to all who came to our home and church. She served as a church deaconess and modeled unconditional love for all she met. Years later, this included befriending Francis, a tall African-American transgendered person who worked with her at Brooklyn College Library. Nobody would associate with Francis, but my mom often invited her for lunches my dad prepared once he retired, with home being a short two-block walk from the library. Hospitality was a demonstration of unconditional love.

3

School

152 IS THE VERY BEST SCHOOL

My local elementary school, Public School (P. S.) 152, located in what was called the Flatbush section of Brooklyn (now Midwood), had a song passed down from generation to generation. It was a song we would sing with gusto at our weekly assemblies:

152 is the very best school,
Twee diddle dee dum bum,
That you can find in Flatbush town,
Twee diddle dee dum bum.
The prettiest girls you ever did see,
The handsomest boys there ever could be,
They all go down to Avenue "G,"
Twee diddle dee dum bum.

Creative variations on the above included the very "worst" school, with the "ugliest girls" substituted by the boys. Us boys identified ourselves as still "handsomest" by comparison, but the girls made similar changes calling us the "ugliest."

My dad also attended P. S. 152 and his name, Albert A. Pazmiño, appears on a large wooden plaque in gold letters at the main entrance, a plaque that includes the names of all the graduates who served in World War II. It made me proud to see his name, generating a sense of familial connection within our neighborhood school. The "A" in his middle name stood for "August." This fact I only learned by digging through family records because my dad opted not to disclose it to me. It is certainly an unusual middle name, and I do not know why his parents gave it to him; I surmised that it was perhaps related to the name of one of Queen Victoria's sons. Although it suggests a different heritage from our Ecuadorean roots. In exploring those roots throughout my life, I have found some suggestion of royalty from my cousin Joseph.

P. S. 152 is an imposing stone building with massive towers, huge glass windows, and a long set of steep stone stairs coming up from Glenwood Road. It reminded me of a castle—a castle of learning inviting all children to enter a new world. It is an unfamiliar setting for us who left the comfortable patterns of family life and daily interactions with neighbors who knew us well. We entered new relationships with teachers and peers while exploring the wonders of the world.

My older sister Laura Lou was in second grade when I started kindergarten. I was so excited to finally attend school. When we often played school at home, she was my domineering teacher. I managed to practice my letters and my first attempt to sound and write out my name produced "Rover" instead of "Robert," resulting in much laughter. I tried my best to improve, managing to print out my name in kindergarten with thick blue (my favorite color) crayon: R-O-B-E-R-T.

Not to be shown up by my sister, I declared to my mother on my first day of kindergarten: "Mom, I will go to school and come home every day all by myself!" I vowed to be independent and not need her help as my sister requested.

Laura Lou was bigger than me and in our fights she always pinned my arms down. I struggled to loosen just one fist, aiming for her nose because she would get nosebleeds. Once I hit her nose,

I quickly ducked away contorting my face to avoid the expected blood drip. She was one of those ugly girls we sang about at school with her bloody nose. I was determined to be better at school than she was by being independent from my mom and getting better grades.

My independent stance led to trouble when a hurricane struck unexpectedly that fall. Once news spread by radio announcements and word of mouth around the neighborhood that school was closing for the storm, parents came to pick up their children.

My usually friendly teacher, Mrs. Fleisch, lost patience after twenty minutes and asked me where my mom was. I sensed her annoyance.

"Please tell me, why isn't she here to pick you up?"

I proudly declared: "I told my mom never to pick me up again after our first day."

As the storm progressed, she wanted to leave and reluctantly released me from school.

Once outside, I slowly progressed around the school building by holding onto the chain link fence that enclosed the playground. With my right hand I gripped the fence and with my left I shielded my face from the pelting rain. After the chain link ended, I grabbed onto the tall metal picket fence surrounding the old section of school along East 23rd Street. When I turned the corner onto Glenwood, the wind suddenly picked up. I held on with both hands and all my strength. I was afraid. I certainly had second thoughts about my independent stance, wondering "Will I ever make it the three short blocks toward Flatbush Avenue?"

Before losing my grip, I heard the familiar voice of our local police officer assigned to our school.

He shouted, "What in the world are you doing out alone in this storm? Where is your mom?"

I repeated what I had told my teacher, now with regret and fear: "I told my mom never to pick me up at school."

He wisely responded: "I appreciate that, but I am taking you home in my squad car. Where do you live?"

In the police car and soaking wet, I reluctantly gave the officer my address, which I had carefully memorized for just such an occasion: "2620 Glenwood Road, Apartment 2E." I wondered if my mom and I were in trouble. I thought, "Will we go to jail?"

Relieved to have arrived safely at the front of my building after a slow drive, I learned that neither my mom nor I were under arrest. I was relieved and began breathing easily again. I also learned it was OK to receive help when needed, especially when storms came.

The same wide sidewalk in front of P. S. 152 was also the scene of another incident from one of my after-school escapades. In sixth grade, I was one of the fastest runners in the school and one of the best punchball players in my class. Most days, after leaving my books at home and having a snack, I would head back down Glenwood Road for a host of pick-up and board games back at school.

Once I arrived in front of my school, I wondered just how fast I could run with my eyes closed. Super heroes accomplish such feats, why not a sixth-grader at the top of his game? Little did I know that I might not be running all that straight! About half-way down the block, I tripped on a protruding sidewalk edge and became airborne. My eyes opened just in time to see the trunk of one of the stately elms lining the block. The right side of my face met that tree in a crushing blow. My face burnt from the collision I somehow thankfully survived. Undeterred, I brushed off my fall and proceeded to my after-school activities. On the way, I dabbed the blood on my face with my ever-ready magic handkerchief known for its miraculous curative powers.

In response to my buddies' inquiries about my facial injury, I bravely said "It's just a scrape!"—a line the cowboys used in movies back then. Of course, I would never have admitted nearly killing myself.

I shared the same response with my mom upon arriving home two hours later. She was unconvinced and marched me into the bathroom to clean my oozing wound. There, in front on the mirror, I was shocked and embarrassed to finally see the extent of the scrape sustained from my close encounter with a tree. I decided then and there never to run again with my eyes closed. I never fully admitted to my classmates how I managed to acquire that bruise, but my son and grandson delight in hearing the retelling of my elementary school memory of running with my eyes closed.

With adult hindsight I realize I could have killed myself. Nevertheless, the scraped face marked me as a tough guy like James Cagney who survived the streets, not admitting my opponent was a tree. The only other time my face was adorned with such a scrape came during my freshman year of college in a required wrestling unit in physical education. I was one of the lightweight students on who my 250-pound wrestling coach selected to demonstrate all new moves. My face made regular encounters with the rough mats. My chosen opponent for the class was a full-bearded Iranian international student who managed to regularly scrape my face to escape holds. Refusing to surrender to his tactic, my face sported the results, but it resulted in an A grade for the course.

Lessons Learned

Independence should be valued up to a point. There are times when we need others to provide wisdom about the real risks of storms and running without looking. When in need, the better course of action is to seek help rather than just brushing it off with misguided bravado. Thankfully, I survived both a hurricane and an encounter with a tree. If injured, it is wise to willingly seek medical help.

JUST IN CASE

With Cold War threats imminent from 1953 to 1960, I was issued a metal dog tag by my school. An ad for a beaded metal chain to accompany my tag read: "A is for Adam, B is for Bomb." This tag would identify me . . . just in case.

The dog tag was blue polished steel, rounded on the corners to prevent irritation under clothing. It had a hole punched on both the far right and left so that a chain or string could be attached. My name was clearly imprinted on the front and my address was pressed neatly in successive centered lines. In the right corner was an inscribed "B," which I thought might be my overall grade in school. I later learned it denoted my blood type. All these means of identification were important . . . just in case. They could save my life.

Duck and cover drills were a critical part of our curriculum. On the appointed day in class, the deafening siren would sound and we would put into practice what we had learned. Any other work was to be immediately stopped and left in place. Our individual oak desk chairs, attached by black iron hinges to the desk behind us, were to be quickly lifted to create space for our crouching bodies. We were to kneel down and make ourselves as small as possible in the limited space. Our arms were to hold our heads tightly, thus protecting our most vulnerable body part. We were also instructed to keep our eyes tightly closed—tightly closed and always facing away from the high glass windows . . . just in case.

New York City was a prime target for launching World War III. Brooklyn was one of the outer boroughs, but those missiles were not all that accurate back then. Even if Manhattan was hit, the ensuing nuclear storm would easily reach P. S. 152 and its large fragile widows. On most days, those windows would bring sunlight, but the light from a nuclear blast would blind us on the spot.

If the bombs hit, time would be precious. Surviving the initial blast would require quick action by using the immediate cover offered by our desks. After the first blast, we would have to line up and descend to the school's basement. Safe basement areas were clearly marked with yellow and black fallout signs. Here is where the blood type noted on our dog tags could mean the difference between life and death. With blood loss, medical staff there could quickly give us the transfusion needed . . . just in case.

Assuming we survived missile attacks, the more menacing threat was the silent killer of polio. Polio lurked in the puddles left after rain. Puddles were always fun to jump in and could be used to douse unsuspecting friends while walking home from school or at recess. Now they could be deadly. The only way to ensure safety was to line up with my school mates for the dreaded shots administered in the same basement rooms designated as fallout shelters. We had to have the all-important permission slips signed by parents. Without a slip, no shot. Without the shot, we were likely headed to life in an iron lung or death. We were only safe once we received all three shots, so life was precarious under the shadow of dreaded polio. Screams could be heard from those who preceded us. Better take a shot and bear the pain . . . just in case.

I wore my dog tag to school every day just in case a bomb or polio had my number. Learning to be careful and live was hard work. Our duck and cover drills along with polio shots broke up any classroom monotony, even when I glanced out the windows into the menacing sky. Those huge windows would no doubt shatter when the Soviets' nuclear bombs hit.

Lessons Learned

Being prepared just in case was a motto not just for the scouts I joined, but for surviving this life. Fears can serve to motivate folk and change behaviors without squelching hope.

MY ELEMENTARY SCHOOL TEACHERS

My elementary teachers were all middle-aged and older women with many years of experience. My sixth grade leather-covered red and white autograph book, with well wishes from all my primary school years, includes notes from some of these teachers, classmates, and friends at graduation. Gratefully, my zippered book survived family moves and my brother's sidewalk sales. Our principal, Dr. Eleanor M. Harrington, in all of her glory with short curly white hair, a huge corsage, smiling while seated at her desk, appears in the front pages. In her photograph, Dr. Harrington has an ominous looking book on her desk, perhaps to record like Santa who was naughty and nice among her wards. My teachers' page listed those who shaped young minds and lives, like mine from 1953 to 1960:

- Kindergarten: Mrs. Fleisch
- 1st Grade: Mrs. Crasson
- 2nd Grade: Mrs. Leonard
- 3rd Grade: Miss Goldstein
- 4th Grade: Mrs. Rosenbluth
- 5th Grade: Mrs. Braun
- 6th Grade: Mrs. Greenway

What I recall from each of my teachers and their classrooms is still surprising me, as my memory has retained experiences and encounters from my formative years, even after many years have passed. Mrs. Fleisch and Mrs. Leonard were not at school when I circulated my autograph book.

Kindergarten

Mrs. Fleisch was energetic and always friendly. That was a good sign for kindergarteners. Our classroom had easy access to an outside playground that was just for us. My favorite apparatus was the "safe" version of the monkey bars, which had metal platforms attached at the base of each of the horizontal openings to prevent us from falling through. It was so unlike the riskier monkey bars found on other city playgrounds that it felt safe; so safe, that once on the top rung, I felt free to kiss one of my cute classmates. Unseen by anyone, I was not disciplined for my amorous indiscretion. What was considered innocent affection back then has become more scrutinized today.

Kindergarten was chock full of activities with pint-sized furniture and brightly colored blocks and paints. Even our bathrooms, which were shared with an adjacent kindergarten class, had smaller fixtures. The setting was a welcoming space to begin my school years. Warm feelings connected learning with others, fun, creativity and the joy of discovery.

One day, the principal Dr. Harrington visited our classroom and asked my teacher to introduce me to her. I was not sure why I was singled out—perhaps due to the aforementioned storm incident or perhaps it was the IQ testing for which my mom had volunteered me at Brooklyn College in the fall of 1953.

The IQ tests took place in a cluster of buildings offering a host of options for play. The massive buildings were also ripe for exploratory ventures—provided we avoided the sometimes-diligent campus security guards on their infrequent rounds. The campus was just one block from both my school and home. It had wide green lawns, numerous practice fields, a goldfish pond, and wide sidewalks uninterrupted by curbs or cross streets ideal for bike and wagon riding.

The opportunity to officially visit a setting generally reserved for play and complete a battery of tests with two college students was a gift. I was even rewarded with the choice of a prize after completing the tests. I selected a small round leather bag made of various leather strips that had a thick black cord to draw it closed tight and keep treasures safe inside. It quickly became the ideal container for my precious marble collection. This was one item, however, that did not survive my brother's sidewalk sale when I went off to college. What did survive was my recollection of one test question that required me to replicate a shape by cutting a carefully folded square of colored paper with round shaped scissors designed for children. I think I cut it wrong and wanted to correct my mistake, but the test continued with the next challenging task testing my skills. From kindergarten with Mrs. Fleisch I discovered the joy of learning through exploration and activity.

First Grade

Mrs. Crasson was strict and demanding, a marked change from the freedom of kindergarten days. In her classroom, each student had an assigned seat and we often had to tightly clasp our hands on our desks when not focused on the numerous tasks assigned to us. Reading, writing, and arithmetic were the order of our day with little time for free play. My class photo shows all the boys decked out in dress pants, white shirts, and even ties, signifying we were ready for the business of real learning. Assigned cubby holes surrounded the classroom, housing our jackets, coats, hats, and gloves in colder months along with the any snacks we had brought: my favorite snack was a dark green box of raisins that were chewy and could be savored over time. Milk, however was provided for us at school. Later in fourth grade I would arrive at school an hour early each day to perform my duties on the prized milk squad. My responsibilities included carrying the individual containers of milk in crates. I took them to each classroom, leaving them in small refrigerators for snack time. I was proud of my service and the special access and status it afforded me. First grade with Mrs. Crasson introduced me to the discipline, order, and focused work required for learning with fun reserved for after school. Her greeting for me was "best wishes" along with her clear signature in my autograph book.

Second Grade

Compared with first grade, second grade with Mrs. Leonard offered a more relaxed change of pace, especially given that she prepped us the day before every test with the answers. I quickly learned her system and I imagine this procedure assured her of having a stellar and high-achieving class, as judged by Dr. Harrington.

Mrs. Leonard was a large woman who did not stray far from her front desk. After leaving apparel in the wardrobe on one side of the class, we socialized across assigned rows, in front and behind our seats. Mrs. Leonard would summon individuals or rows to come to her desk to receive our assignments or to submit competed work. She permitted talking and interaction as we assisted each other with our assignments when needed.

Penmanship was the most highly-prized subject. Mrs. Leonard used a long pointer with a black tip to emphasize how each letter was to be formed using the array of capital and lowercase letters pictured across the front of the classroom. Good work was rewarded with a note and visit to the principal's office for Dr. Harrington's praise. I took that trip on a few occasions.

From second grade with Mrs. Leonard I learned the value of clear communication through careful penmanship and the possibilities of cooperative and collaborative learning with peers. Unfortunately, her signature does not appear in my book to check out her penmanship after these many years.

Third Grade

Riding high from second grade's easy successes, I had a rude awakening upon entering third grade. Miss Goldstein, white haired, looked old and mean, wearing a scowl on her face most days. She asked us on our first day: "Who would like to read for us from our new readers?" Mine was one of the first hands raised. I always volunteered with enthusiasm to demonstrate my academic skills.

Miss Goldstein called on me: "You can turn to the back of the book and start reading the last chapter." Every third word was new to me and I stammered my way through, having to sound out each unknown word. Halfway through the long third sentence, she said with subdued anger and obvious disgust, "That is enough. Now sit down." Totally embarrassed, I sheepishly sat back down.

The next pupil to be called upon was a precocious girl. Strategically, Miss Goldstein asked her to turn back to the *front* of the book. The girl read well. I could have easily done that if given a similarly easy passage.

"Why did she have me read from the back of the book?"

After school friends told me that my teacher had a reputation for hating boys. Despite this knowledge, my first experience with failure affected my school performance. My third-grade report card without the usual outstanding designations confirmed my suspicion. All the girls in that class teased the boys about their comparatively stellar report cards. This was the case even when our test scores were notably higher. Reverse gender discrimination, while unusual for that time, was certainly informative. Four years later when I graduated primary school, Miss Sarah Goldstein signed my autograph book with "best wishes." I imagine "best, but guarded" from my humbling experience in third grade.

Fourth Grade

Fourth grade brought yet another radical change when I became the teacher's pet. Mrs. Rosenbluth was a joyful spirit who often had us sing in class. She called on me for all special assignments, such as taking messages to the main office. She even recognized before peers my stellar work. I won all the book prizes that year (including *Island Boy*, which I loved), relishing the special attention. That book stirred my imagination of a carefree life beyond the crowded apartment buildings and tough city streets that called for constant diligence. One could be surprised by marauding gangs who stole bikes and any precious cash one had saved for trips to local candy stores, Woolworths or Kresge's Five and Ten Cent Store on Flatbush Avenue. *Island Boy*, as the title implies, recounted the adventurous life of a boy my age as he explored his world and met new friends.

With the death of my older brother at birth, Albert Pazmiño Jr., a twin to Laura Lou, I was to be the school achiever for my immediate family. I always wondered what it would be like to have an older brother, but somehow knew that under my different circumstances, I was expected to be "the successful son." Ultimately, what Mrs. Rosenbluth did was recognize my potential for success. My peers recognized the status I had earned in the classroom, which filtered into the schoolyard, where I always played to win. Mrs. Rosenbluth's entry in my autograph book was "You are bound to be a success because you are so very fine." Her affirmation encouraged me to do well in school from that time forward.

Fifth Grade

Fifth grade did not sustain my high-profile status with Mrs. Braun, whom I recall as being competent, but most days depressed. Advanced skills and subjects were covered to prepare us for sixth grade, but joy came with peer interactions during class when Mrs. Braun was readily distracted. Carefully crafted spitballs launched across the room with rulers and notes meticulously worked through the crevices of attached rows of wooden desks occupied the times between daily assignments and Fridays' tests. Mrs. Braun was nearly blind and we delighted in managing to avoid being caught passing answers to our tests when any neighbors encountered an impasse. If the class became too unruly, Mrs. Braun had her favorite scapegoats, who usually were the ones instigating the mayhem. Tommy Di always had the wisecrack that resulted in a trip to the principal's office with a roar of laughter.

Our laughter brought the wrath of Mrs. Brennan, whose class met just across the hall. She was a large imposing woman with dark hair and a stern expression that engendered fear in the hearts of all students. She was known as the self-appointed disciplinarian on the floor. Once Mrs. Brennan came into our classroom to support her beleaguered colleague, all frolicking immediately ceased. Her voice boomed, "Settle down! Stop it!" If unheeded, the culprit was personally carted off to the principal's office by Mrs. Brennan.

At the end of fifth grade I had my own run-in with Mrs. Brennan. Serving on the AAA Crossing Guard Squad was a cherished responsibility. Early every morning before school, and in the afternoon following classes, boys on the squad were posted at key crosswalks to assist younger students. I was assigned to a key crosswalk at Glenwood and East 23rd Street. My perfect attendance, diligence, and effective service meant I was in line to be the honored captain of the squad in sixth grade.

On the fateful sunny spring afternoon after a late recess with all fifth grade classes outside, my squad buddies and I were headed to our posts, when we were distracted by a chance to socialize with some of the prettiest girls in our grade, who were lined up on the inside of the school fence. Mrs. Brennan spotted us.

"How dare you stop to talk with girls when you all should be at your assigned posts?"

We were then instructed to report back to her immediately after our duties. Mrs. Brennan had arranged a meeting with the kind and well-loved Mr. Garibaldi, who supervised the squad. Once he was informed of our transgression, I was informed on the spot, "Sorry Robert, you cannot serve as the squad captain next year. You were in line for that job, but not now."

I was devastated, but learned the seriousness of being responsible from fifth grade. Mrs. Braun signed her "best wishes" and signature, but on a distinct angle in my book reflecting her sight challenge.

Sixth Grade

Even with my crossing squad demotion, sixth grade was the crowning achievement of my elementary school years with my graduation taking place on June 29, 1960, after a year of perfect attendance. Each day that year began with the class gathering and facing the rear blackboard to recite our motto "Aim for the stars, and you may reach the treetops." We all wrote that motto into our autograph books and Mrs. Greenway signed and dated it June 27, 1960.

We worked hard that last year and were rewarded with a visit from Reverend Greenway, Mrs. Greenway's husband. We had studied the Civil War and the legacy of Abraham Lincoln. Rev. Greenway, who pastored a nearby church, was in possession of a prized death mask of President Lincoln. He told us all the amazing story of how he acquired the plaster mask and what Lincoln's life meant to him. The mask was carefully wrapped and packed in a heavy metal case with thick yellow foam cushions on all sides. He encouraged us to live a worthy life of service to others following President Lincoln's stellar example and I suppose his as well.

Lessons learned

My teachers at P. S. 152, whom some in my neighborhood had dubbed "old biddies," nevertheless inspired me to consider teaching as my life's vocation. Reciting the pledge of allegiance each morning was a common ritual in each of their classrooms from kindergarten through sixth grade. I learned from their good and not so good examples of the potentials and pitfalls of teaching and learning. The opportunity to care for and shape others' lives is a high calling that has been my life's work and joy.

ANDRIES HUDDE

My first day at Junior High School (J. H. S.) 240, known as "Andries Hudde," in September 1960 coincided with the remains of a hurricane that swept through New York.

"Was this a sign of what adolescence would bring?" I wondered.

For the first time in my life I had to travel to school by public bus. My sister Laura Lou reluctantly told me what to expect in buses jam-packed with students. Even a short ride to Nostrand Avenue and Avenue K was a momentous change from the three-block walk to P. S. 152. I feared being bullied by those gang members known to extort money and any objects worth the taking from unsuspecting seventh graders. I was warned to stick with groups and avoid standing out too much, except to impress teachers in my classes. Having more than one teacher and changing classrooms for each subject was also very new to me, and initially intimidating, but it offered a chance to learn from teachers who were passionate about their particular subjects.

I had new clothes for the start of a new year and even a raincoat to weather the day, all bought at the Sears Roebuck department store down on Bedford Avenue. I wore gray chino pants that had a small, stylish fabric belt just over the rear pockets, and a button-down pale yellow shirt. I remembered to generously use my Mennen Speed Stick deodorant (same as my dad's), since my body was maturing. My goal was to begin the special three-year program (S. P. 3) on the right foot, impressing others with both my academic brilliance and athletic skills. The academic program was special because it grouped academically gifted students together for all classes for three intense and enriched years of study. Back at P. S. 152 I was a mainstay on the honor roll and one of the best runners and punchball players in the school.

Junior high also presented my first opportunity to go out for lunch and use my own money to purchase whatever I desired at one of the nearby candy stores, which had counter service with the menus posted overhead on an ever-changing board. This was just like my dad would do in Manhattan the times I went to lunch with him. This was a big deal and a foray into the adult world of increased independence.

I was the only one in my homeroom class to opt to leave the school building on my first day, a rain-drenched day. Peers asked, "You really going out for lunch with all the rain? Man, are you crazy?" This did not deter me. I had the freedom to go out for lunch and I was going to experience it and no rain could squelch my enthusiasm and newfound privilege.

I used all my strength to push open the heavy school doors on Avenue K buffeted by strong winds. Within a few steps, I was soaked even with my raincoat buttoned up, and could hardly see my destination across the street. Leaping across wide puddles and ruining my new suede shoes in the process, I finally made it into the dark, cramped space of the candy store, which had just one open seat at the counter. Only one other student dared this outing and he was just leaving with a candy bar in hand. He was my height, so I imagined he was in seventh grade. But he did ask:

"What grade are you in?"

"Seventh" was my sheepish reply.

"I'm in ninth. I hate that school and wish I was already in high school," were his fleeting words of discouragement.

Not deterred, I turned to the counter man as he barked:

"What do you want, kid?"

I was technically no longer a kid, now that I was twelve and in junior high. Didn't he notice?

Glancing quickly at the board I said: "Tuna on rye with a pickle please."

"For here or to go?"

Not relishing eating a soaked sandwich in wet clothes at school, I confidently said, "Here."

Given the price of the sandwich, I opted for water and not my favorite cherry coke. Freedom came with a price. I gulped down my lunch and vowed not to exercise all my independence in the days ahead. In hindsight, I missed having lunch with all my new classmates and exploring the cafeteria offerings, which I later learned were not all that bad, less costly and in bigger portions than what I could afford on my weekly one-dollar allowance and any additional earnings I made from babysitting. The cost of the bus, even with my reduced-fare school bus pass, was a nickel each way and the option of bringing my lunch was increasingly attractive with Fridays reserved for buying lunch in the school cafeteria to end the week with a special treat of a large tuna hero sandwich.

Four days a week I prepared my own lunch. I relished making a variety of sandwiches including salami, liverwurst with mustard, tuna, ham and cheese with mayo and, only as a last resort, bologna, if the standby peanut butter and jelly were depleted. By junior high there were three other siblings vying for lunch options. Apart from Laura Lou, who was two years ahead of me, Ronnie and Lisa had come along, seven and eleven years after I arrived on the Brooklyn scene.

I enjoyed having younger siblings and caring for them when I was not outside playing ball, doing homework, or at scouts. The skills I learned from caring for Ronnie and Lisa had the immediate payoff: I was able to earn money through babysitting the younger children of church families who trusted me without question. Usually Laura Lou was asked first, but I was next in line and actually preferred caring for boys like Scott and Shawn, whose parents were Rosie and Brian Howard. Rosie was Portuguese and Brian was Irish and they were always fun to be around. Our church attracted folks from unique ethnic and cultural backgrounds that, in my case, included Ecuadorean and Double Dutch roots.

I remember Rosie had darker skin that attracted public scrutiny when Pastor Fred Gibson took us all for a beach outing at the private Breezy Point Community with an invitation he had received as a local clergyman. It was a beautiful mid-July day ideal for the beach. The gate attendant did look sheepish when the pastor shared his invitation card as he spied all passengers. Breezy Point, unknown to me, was a segregated community and our presence posed a threat. Pastor knew of racism from his southern roots and had studied with Martin Luther King Jr. at Crozier Theological Seminary in Philadelphia. We were surprised after setting up our blankets on the pristine sand to be quickly approached by the community security who was informed by the gate attendant.

"Hello, officer. Can I help you?" offered the pastor.

"Your kind are not welcome here!" I overheard the officer say, even at a distance.

"Just what kind is that?" Pastor Fred asked with a frown appearing on his face.

"This is a private beach and we set restrictions on who can visit and bathe here."

"I am a local minister and have been invited with my friends to visit."

"I am sure your host was not aware of who exactly was coming. Either you leave right now or I will call local police to escort you all out! What is it going to be, you leave voluntarily or by force?"

Once Rosie learned of the problem, she had us gather up everything and move quickly to the wood-paneled Ford station wagon in which we had come.

Pastor Fred was apologetic, "Rosie, I am so sorry this has happened."

She suggested, "Let's all just go to Riis Park, it's nearby and we can still enjoy the day!"

"This is what I want to fight against here up north as well as down south, but not today with you all here," Pastor Fred reflected as we exited the community's gates. I was tempted to throw a middle finger to the gate attendant, but thought better of it given the younger children present.

I had learned in Mrs. Bragan's social studies class about racism and its effects on people, but never experienced firsthand until that summer day at Breezy Point. (By the way, Mrs. Bragan signed my junior high autograph book: "I wish you all the very best that life has to offer. It has been a joy being your teacher. My only regret is that you are leaving. Oh! For a class full of Roberts!") Connections emerged for the toll hatred could take, especially on children, much more than any toll paid to cross the Marine Park Bridge that brought us to Breezy Point.

"What had led white folks to exclude any dark-skinned persons from their community and right here in New York, where people came from all around the globe? Could this really be happening to us and to Rosie, who was so nice and attractive? This is sick and no wonder black folks are pushing for change," I thought that night as I tried to make sense of the day's events. Pastor Fred preached and taught alternatives to our multiracial and multiethnic congregation and lived them out. Folks from all backgrounds were welcomed and appreciated at Kenilworth Baptist and the pastor modeled what Jesus taught about loving our neighbors, whoever they might be. Those neighbors could become close friends.

In junior high I met George Marmorino who quickly became my best friend throughout adolescence, even though he opted to attend Brooklyn Tech for high school. George was also a good student, an athlete, and had Hispanic roots through his vivacious Puerto Rican mom. George was the youngest of four siblings with three older sisters to my one; all of them lived outside of his home. George's dad was an Italian salesman who spent most of his time on the road, so it was often just George and his mom. George's dad had an amazing coin collection, which he kept in a gated vault in the basement of their attached private home. George loved spending time with my family, including our summer car trips to upstate destinations.

George and I idealized the Greek culture about which we learned even to the extent of jointly buying a hard-rubber practice discus that we tossed at Riis Park off-season. We built bonfires from driftwood after trying polar-bear dips in the ocean like real Spartan men in training. Steve Reeves who played the muscle-bound hero in numerous films became our idol fueled by Saturday viewings at the Marine and Brook Theatres down on Flatbush Avenue.

The one teacher who contacted both George and me after many years was our math teacher Miss Bialer who later married our art teacher Mr. Tritt. George and I had a typical junior high crush on her and were so disappointed when she didn't wait until we were of marrying age. She remembered George and me as being "shining stars." Both of the Tritts contributed much to others in their educational careers, serving across the country as principals and superintendents. Miss Bialer, now Mrs. Tritt, signed my autograph book: "It has been very enjoyable this term and I wish you could be here again. I am sure that you do well in all that you try— so I will wish you happiness rather than luck. I do hope you will return and let us know of your whereabouts and doings—again, it has been a pleasure."

Lessons Learned

The real world is less than ideal, including my encounter with racism. Gates can protect coins, but exclude people. Problems can divide different people, and Christian faith along with other faiths can work for the formation of a beloved community on the small scale of a local church and perhaps over time in the wider community. Pastor Fred was a better role model than Steve Reeves for what was important, possible, and sustainable in my life. After leaving our congregation, Fred became the Protestant chaplain at Richmond University and even served as a missionary university chaplain in Singapore. Caring for others may require crossing borders and entering gates of exclusion with the hope of teaching and living into new ways. Having friends while taking risks and learning together helps along the way of maturing.

MIDWOOD HIGH SCHOOL

My cousin Kenneth DeMay and I both attended Midwood High School in Brooklyn. He was fifteen years older than I was. Kenneth later became a nationally known architect and I spoke at his memorial service in 2010 on behalf of the family about his life's legacy. A legacy he passed on to me from Midwood was his vintage high school jacket that Ken's mom, my beloved Aunt Stella, shared with me. I enjoyed wearing his Midwood jacket—everyone admired when I wore it. The jacket had affixed to it his letter for the rifle team that in 1963 still existed, but was not well known.

Midwood was located just one block from my apartment building, so I could literally roll out of bed and after gulping breakfast be in class in record time. Record times were important because I was a member of both the high school cross-country and track teams during my junior year until my fateful concussion suffered in the early Spring of 1965. In the fall of 1965 our cross-country team won the all-city "C" division team championship at Van Cortland Park in the Bronx where three hundred runners converged across a wide field to enter the narrow course just two abreast.

It was a cool and overcast Saturday afternoon during a pick-up touch football game at the schoolyard when my accident occurred. We had passed off after I scored a touchdown and the football traveled the required yardage where we could recover it. I was racing full speed and had the ball scooped up while in a hunched position. A heavy lineman defender extended his elbow just enough to catch my head as I was standing up to make my quick move in advancing the recovered ball. I was knocked unconscious on the spot and awoke to a world set at an angle. With time on the sidelines, my vision returned to normal, but I never thought I needed medical assistance. From that blow my whole body felt depressed and weak and I was out of sorts when I returned to school with headaches and loss of interest.

During that time I was also practicing for the track team and pushing myself to achieve as I had done in all my school subjects.

I had the goal of going to an Ivy League college like all of the high achievers in my special math-science program for the Midwood intellectual elite. I was a member of the math team and prided myself in also being athletic. I pushed myself to exhaustion and experienced a mini-depression until learning that I had sustained a concussion. Missing six weeks of my junior year was a disaster for college applications, but the support of my family and a math tutor made all the difference. Life was less than the classic ideals that George Marmorino and I had embraced in junior high, but I could go even if the Ivy League setting was not all that it was promoted in my mind to be. The internist who diagnosed my concussion said it best:

"Robert, you have recovered from your head blow and concussion. You can now return to school after your extended rest with no fear. You know, it is OK if you don't go to an Ivy League school. I didn't and have succeeded in my profession. You will do well wherever you attend college. Now get out of here and get on with your life."

His advice was timely to put things into perspective and to strive to do my best, rather than what others thought was best for me. I left the track team and opted to be the manager of the cross-country team rather than run during my senior year given my internist's wise recommendations.

During my high school years, the modeling and support of Pastor Fred made a difference. Given that my parents had not completed college, he took the time to ask me about my plans for college and encouraged me to consider schools with Baptist roots, which included Bucknell University in Lewisburg, Pennsylvania along with Brown University in Providence, Rhode Island. David Chichester, whom I knew from childhood, attended Brown and I visited there during my junior year, along with Princeton where Jack Cumming, my Sunday school teacher, had attended.

Pastor Fred also decided to take me and two friends for a day's visit to the Franklin Institute in Philadelphia. He drove us past Crozier Theological Seminary where he had attended along with Martin Luther King Jr., who was increasingly in the news.

We had a blast together and his interest in us and our lives affirmed our search to find meaning in the increasingly confused and changing world the sixties brought.

My college applications were submitted to Brown, Lawrence University nearby where my sister studied at Potsdam State College, and Clarkson where my soon-to-be brother-in-law attended, and Bucknell. Fortunately I applied to college during the boom years of President Johnson's administration when financial resources for poorer city students abounded with presidential scholarships. That generous support along with scholarships from the City of New York's Mayor, Eastern Star, and my local church meant that I could afford college. Once I visited Bucknell and fell in love with the small town setting as an alternative to the city of Providence, I headed back to my mother's home state with a stated interest in majoring in geology. Geology also offered the possibility of spending time outdoors and exploring new areas of the world that stirred my youthful imagination.

Lessons Learned

Despite setbacks like concussions, life can continue with options beyond long-cherished expectations like Ivy League colleges. The support of others sustains us in times of transitions and struggle.

REFLECTIONS ON SCHOOL

Given the many years I have spent in schools at various levels, education has been a key formative setting and influence in my life. What was it about schools that so fascinated my vocational imagination and life work?

School at the elementary and secondary levels was where I most fulfilled family expectations of achievement during my formative years. Being the oldest surviving male child of my parents, I was groomed for great academic accomplishments. My mom noted what the nurses at Methodist Hospital said when first presenting me to her at birth: "Here is your professor!" Little did they know that this newborn would come to invest his life in service by teaching others in theological schools.

Later in her life, my mom mentioned that, when my older brother Albert died at birth as a twin to my surviving sister, she had prayed as Hannah from the Old Testament did. Hannah, then childless, prayed God would give her a son. If so blessed, she promised to dedicate the son whom she would name Samuel to the service of God. My mother prayed that same prayer and dedicated me, prior to conception, to God's service. I was however, called to serve in theological schools, which I have done for thirty plus years, fulfilling the promise she made in my early life.

My mother later anticipated that I would serve as a physician given my interest in math and science in secondary school, instead of exploring and teaching in the field of Christian education.

Schools represent a place for the development of the mind, spirit, character, and work habits of individuals. They also play a crucial formative role for the whole of life. Schools as a formal aspect of education need to work in complementary ways with the informal and non-formal dimensions of education for the shaping of lives, families, groups, communities, and societies in transformative ways. They serve to foster the potential and imagination of students who aim for the stars and climb on trees while avoiding running into them.

4

Church

FIRST GLIMPSES OF GOD

Glimpses of God were nurtured initially in my home and then nurtured by my local church. In my case, those glimpses took shape in church-related camp settings sponsored by Kenilworth Baptist Church located just one city block from my apartment building. Teachers and pastors of that church and my parents supported and prayed for me and enabled me to attend summer church camps.

Apartment 2E, 2620 Glenwood Road, Brooklyn, New York— June 1949

My earliest memory comes when I close my eyes and drift back to the well of experience imprinted on my life. I know it is summer time because the windows are open in the one bedroom of my family's apartment. I am comfortably lying on my back in a crib and feel a breeze blowing across my face even as the sun streams in, brightly filling the room with a fullness I want to embrace.

The breeze invites the sheer long curtain to playfully dance across the top of the white wicker crib as it responds to the flow of fresh air that gives a slight hint of sea. I sense a presence with me that bring a state of contentment and joy, along with longing for the unexpected.

The researcher Edward Robinson writes about such an encounter in *The Original Vision* that describes children's experience of the numinous, of God. I later discover as an adult that I am a visual learner, thus my earliest memory provided an entry point for my sense of wonder and awe. When writing and thinking, I often look up to see what patterns can be discerned and shared with others, enabling us to glorify and enjoy God now and forever. I am awaiting the cool breeze of God's Spirit to enter the windows of our souls assuring us that we are God's beloved for all time. We are God's beloved despite all we may encounter in life's journey.

Metropolitan Baptist Camp, Poughquag, New York —July 1957

The first glimpse of the joyous light of God's creation of which I was instantly cognizant came when I was nine years old, a tough city boy from Brooklyn. That summer I went to Metropolitan Baptist Camp in Poughquag, New York. One bright morning all the campers hiked up Mount Dennis, and from its tree-less mountain top we saw laid out before us the awesome sight of three states and a wide expanse of deep blue sky and densely wooded mountains. After sitting quietly to observe that amazing view and bask in the bright sun, we all sang "This is my father's world" as we saw God's creation visible before us:

> This is my Father's world and to my listening ears
> all nature sings and round me rings the music of the spheres.
> This is my Father's world: I rest me in the thought
> of rocks and trees, of skies and seas;
> his hand the wonders wrought.

Tears of joy and wonder ran down my face as I saw God's light for the second time in my childhood. I wiped those tears away quickly so as not to be seen by others. Like the shepherd boy David, as described in the Bible storybook given to me by Reddy, I paused to see God's glorious light made plain before my eyes and spirit outside the city.

Metropolitan Baptist Camp—August 16, 1966

I carry in my wallet still to this day a well-worn picture of Jesus portrayed as praying in the Garden of Gethsemane at night. He is kneeling on a rocky, thorn-lined ledge, with his arms outstretched and clasped in prayer. Wearing a white tunic under a navy blue robe with a crimson red lining, Jesus has long hair and a full beard and looks to be about thirty years of age. But his head is not bowed. Instead he is looking up into the heavens and peering at a numinous cloud that might be illuminated by the moon.

On the back of the picture I affixed the date of August 16, 1966, and the following inscription: "To Christ I have given my life. He entered my heart and changed my life. I am to thank him always." To that, I added my signature. I am always careful to add the tilde to my last name to celebrate my Ecuadorean heritage.

What happened on August 16th, 1966? This memory, given its significance and though first recalled under border-crossing, is worth revisiting for its spiritual meaning. I was being called to be open to God's love and the love of a young woman.

The summer of 1966 was the second year I worked as a camp counselor. That year, I was the counselor for the junior and senior high campers after I had just graduated from Midwood High School in June. It was serendipitous that Wanda Melendez was assigned as my female complement. When I first met Wanda for counselor training, I was immediately attracted to this Latina beauty, who reminded me of the actress Natalie Wood—best known for her role as María in *West Side Story*. Like María, Wanda lived in Spanish Harlem. After living there, she moved to Puerto Rico for three years, before moving to the Bronx.

My initial interest in Wanda was rebuffed. She announced to me and others at a roadside rest stop after a counselors' trip orientation to Manhattan that "I don't like you, even though we will be working together this summer!"

"So much for a budding summer romance before heading off to Bucknell University in the fall," I thought to myself. But, my verbal response, "I was just trying to be helpful because I was a counselor last year."

Things changed over the course of the summer and, one late July afternoon as we were coming back from Lake Dennis and cool winds were blowing, Wanda confided to me as we cowered under our beach towels, "I know someone who can keep me warm!" She was looking directly at me with her beautiful dark eyes, and fortunately, I took her cue, cautiously wrapping my arm around her shoulder as we walked through the woods back to our platform tents with all of our cold campers in tow.

After that walk, Wanda and I spent any spare minute in each other's company and I knew in my heart that I met the woman I wanted to marry, despite that she was also my first real girlfriend. When I announced my intentions to my parents, they quickly made a trip up to camp to meet the love of my life. On our subsequent return to the city, both families met.

One difference between us was the evangelical Baptist faith that Wanda and her family embraced and my more progressive Baptist roots. Wanda spoke of the need to personally commit one's life to follow Christ, whereas I sought to follow Christian ways of living at an arm's distance. I had even refused adult baptism with all the questions I had at the age of thirteen about becoming a Christian follower.

I did recall the camp visit of Pastor Bob Santilli, who spoke of the need for this commitment during a service for the counselors, but struggled all summer to figure out how that might relate to me.

Near summer's end, Wanda and I were sitting alone in Pell Lodge at the camp before a huge stone fireplace that had a hand-carved, wooden cross displayed on the mantle. In focusing upon the cross, I realized that Jesus' life and death offered me a gift and a new life requiring my faith in response. I recognized the need for sins to be forgiven and God's gracious provision of a remedy in Jesus Christ. What overwhelmed me was the realization that he was willing to die upon the cross for my sins, for me, and offered new life. God's love in Christ called for a response of my love and life commitment to follow Jesus as his disciple.

I made that commitment and tears began to uncontrollably stream down my face. A tough youth from Brooklyn was not supposed to cry, especially not in the presence of his new girlfriend. Wanda tenderly assured me of God's love for me and her love as well, which overwhelmed me in a time of transition with college on the horizon. Exactly three years later on August 16, 1969 Wanda and I wed. What was it about this camp setting that now tugged upon my heart yet again?

Lessons Learned

Glimpses of God can serve to define one's life. This was the case for me. The search for meaning is navigated through relationships with others this side of heaven.

SUNDAY SCHOOL

From my earliest memories, every Sunday morning my mom, older sister, and I attended Sunday school at Kenilworth Baptist Church, which were followed by worship services when I was old enough to read and sit relatively still. Until the age of seven, the three of us would walk along the long triangular city block of Amersfort Place to where it intersected with Kenilworth and East 26th Street. There at the very pinnacle of the triangle, sat a small white church building with a prominent bell steeple that seemed better fit to a New England town than an interfaith neighborhood in Brooklyn. But then the Brooklyn of my youth was known as the "borough of churches," and churches come in a variety of forms and traditions.

At the age of eight, I would ring the bell attached to a thick rope tethered near the last pew of the sanctuary on the right as you entered. The rope was secured around a thick brass hook, and when pulled, moved up and down into the ceiling as the bell tolled, welcoming the neighborhood to worship in the American Baptist tradition that welcomed all.

The sanctuary was seamlessly connected to the educational wing with its upstairs apartment for our pastor and his family. Under the sanctuary was a huge basement ideal for indoor games and the scout meetings I regularly attended. I progressed through the cub scouts, boy scouts, and explorers as I passed through my later childhood and adolescence. Scouts and church were closely allied in the formation of boys like me in our journey to manhood. If the weather was bad, our dad would drive us to church as he did for a number of older church members who needed rides. I imagined my dad's former Catholic affiliation meant he opted out of attending a Protestant, and particularly Baptist, church. My mom had longstanding Baptist roots and she intended for us to embrace her faith from birth on. My dad's distance from church radically changed when I was seven.

My dad began meeting with our pastor, Rev. David Jester at that time, and he made a faith commitment to follow Jesus when I was seven years old. That commitment meant he attended church with us, rather than just dropping us off. I sensed the family was more whole and Sunday meals from then on often included pastor and his family as well. All of our pastors were men in those days, though women, like my mom, served as deaconesses and informally ran church activities and outreach. The pastoral family was added to the usual invited guests in our home, but anyone who did not have a place for Sunday dinner was welcome. These meals, given my dad's love of cooking and mom's love of hospitality, were a major weekly event, requiring all hands on deck to assist in serving our guests and making them feel at home when sitting at the bounteous table. The spread on those Sundays fueled us up for each challenging week at school, my dad's office, or the household, where my mom, when well, provided an oasis in the city.

My mom did struggle with occasional ulcers, which required her hospitalization when my older sister and I were in adolescence. Those occasions called us to care for our younger siblings, assisted by our Great Aunt Eloisa who was strict and demanding. Though never married and without her own children, Aunt Eloisa had clear expectations of how children ought to properly behave.

"Polite children are expected to carefully chew their food with their mouths tightly closed," she reminded before each meal.

"Conversation during meals should avoid any silliness, and loud laughing at the table does not show good manners!"

My mom often served as a teacher for young children at Sunday school when I was a preschooler. My younger brother and sister followed the family ritual of church attendance when they came along seven and eleven years later.

Mrs. Ferguson was the superintendent who led our opening exercises before we divided into separate classes based on age. We all sat in the largest room before a life-size painting of Jesus, who was portrayed with long hair, a full beard, a white rope with a blue sash, set in a lush garden and knocking at a door at twilight. This portrayal suggested that Jesus sought entrance into the doors of our lives, beckoning us to follow him all our days. Each week we sang accompanied by Mildred Trim playing the piano with gusto, and smiled with enthusiasm:

> Jesus loves me this I know
> For the Bible tells me so.
> Little ones to him belong.
> They are weak, but he is strong.
> Yes, Jesus loves me.
> Yes, Jesus loves me.
> Yes, Jesus loves me.
> The Bible tells me so.

Mrs. Ferguson had the habit of placing her tongue between her front teeth and lower lip and covering her mouth with her right hand between her sentences. This habit was curious in unintentionally gaining our attention, as we would perk up to listen to what she might say. In contrast to Mildred, she did not smile with her noticeable disability. Later in life, I realized an intentional revision of song lyrics that Mrs. Ferguson taught in keeping with her Christian pacifist stance. With all the appropriate body motions she taught us the following song:

> I *will* never march in the infantry (marching in place)
> Ride in the cavalry (holding reigns of our horses)
> Shoot the artillery (holding with both hands a machine gun firing rounds)
> I *will* never zoom o'er the enemy (arms extended as if flying)
> Cause I'm (pointing to ourselves) in the Lord's army (pointing heavenward),
> Cause I'm in the Lord's army,
> And I *will* never . . .

Mildred played enthusiastically while we all used our arms and legs in tune with the song and its active lyrics. The usual version of that Sunday school favorite used the word "may" in place of the "will" Mrs. Ferguson substituted. Some fathers, like mine, had prior military service, but we were taught about the alternative if we were to serve faithfully in the Lord's Christian army. I wonder if those early lessons influenced my decision to volunteer for the Navy's medical corps when drafted to serve in the Vietnam War in 1970, which is explored in the epilogue.

A remarkable series of Sunday school teachers did their best to instruct an always-questioning student like myself. Mrs. Tabitha Taylor, who lived in an apartment over the Pizza Den on Flatbush Avenue, with her dark hair all pinned up and dark glasses did her best to laugh at my jokes and commend my outlandish inquiries. Tabby Taylor had to be a saint to live with Bill, her husband. Bill was a good friend of my dad's and a bowling buddy on the church's league team. Bill never stopped talking loudly and was an expert on any conversation topic, even if he knew nothing about it. Later, after Tabby died, he was a regular visitor at our home. He was one I sought to avoid by announcing homework I needed to complete or studying for an upcoming test after extended Sunday meals. My parents modeled a gracious patience with any lonely and hurting visitor, which still astounds me to this day. But Bill did something right in fathering Eleanor, who was a sweet, beautiful, blond young woman who also became my Sunday school teacher.

Eleanor had high expectations that we would memorize Bible verses each week to demonstrate our commitment to learning about God. With such a challenge and having a crush, I searched both Testaments of the Bible. I discovered John 11:35 (KJV) "Jesus wept;" 1 Thessalonians 5:16 (KJV) "Rejoice evermore;" and the very next verse from 1 Thessalonians 5:17 (KJV) "Pray without ceasing." I discovered the shortest biblical verses. Though Eleanor was somewhat pleased, rewarding me with a smile for my diligence, I received the best laughs from my peers in that class who settled for longer verses. The biggest disappointment came when it was announced that Eleanor was engaged to Dan, the church organist and choir director. "What a waste!" I had secretly thought that Eleanor would wait and marry me some day, but that did not happen.

Next in line of teachers was Nancy Simms, who had a genuine and deep personal interest in each of her students. Her roots went back to the coal-mining country of eastern Pennsylvania, from where several other church families, like the Ritz clan, came. Nancy baked a cake for each of our birthdays, which was shared during class, and she even asked the week before about our favorite flavors. Her care contrasted with the normal fare of public schools. A Sunday school class of four to six students developed a close sense of community that I looked forward to renewing each week. That care was recognized at the end of each year with the reward of perfect attendance pins for Sunday school participation, designated with successive numbers. Those pins were worn at the Brooklyn day parade when each church had a decorated float and marched down Bedford Avenue.

At the age of thirteen, baptism classes were held to prepare candidates entering adult church membership. My sister Laura Lou and I were enrolled along with peers, and the pastor at that time was our teacher. After the instruction, we were given the option to join the church followed by baptism via immersion in the church's tank. The tank was usually hidden under wooden planks in the sanctuary and only filled for baptisms. My sister opted to proceed, but I chose to wait with the many questions I had about the Christian faith. Despite these questions, I continued to regularly attend both Sunday school and church and, during my senior year in high school, even served as the kindergarten teacher. Along with my teaching, my mom and I also sang in the church's choir that was enjoyable each week.

During high school, my Sunday school teacher was Jack Cumming. Jack and his wife Marianne lived just down the block from the church on Kenilworth Place near Glenwood Road. Jack was a graduate of Princeton University and he challenged his students to learn the roots of the Christian faith. Together we read and discussed the book *The Church of Our Fathers* by Roland H. Bainton, which traces the history of the Christian church from its very beginnings in the first century. Jack also arranged a trip to Princeton with Mark Rodin and me who were hoping to attend college. We went to a football game and dined at the eating club where Jack had been a member during his college years. What was most memorable from the meal were the African American servants who lined the dining room walls, while all the white members and guests sat at the tables. The servants wore white jackets and gloves and avoided any eye contact with those whom they were serving. This meal was so unlike the church suppers where all seated together, with servers and diners from all races and backgrounds mingling, laughing, and sharing the stories of our lives. In addition to our reading, Jack required each of his students to write a paper on a topic of interest from church history. He encouraged us to improve our research and writing skills in preparation for college.

Lessons Learned

One chorus we often repeated at Kenilworth Baptist's Sunday School, with Mrs. Ferguson leading and Mildred Trim on the piano, was:

> A sunbeam, a sunbeam
> Jesus wants me for a sunbeam.
> A sunbeam, a sunbeam,
> I'll be a sunbeam for him.

When I recall my earliest glimpse of God, it was the sunbeams that played with a sheer curtain dancing over the top of my crib. My life vocation has been to be a sunbeam for Jesus in the theological field of Christian education. I hope others can experience the playful light of the gospel in the lives of their Sunday school teachers across the globe and across the ages. My mother had prayed at the death of my older brother Albert for her next-born son to be used by God, and that prayer has been answered in my life's vocation. My Sunday school teachers modeled a genuine concern and care for their students along with what they taught about the Christian faith.

BROOKLYN DAY PARADE

Brooklyn was known as the borough of churches and the public school holiday of Brooklyn Day celebrated the history and influence of Sunday schools in the lives of local citizens. Every local church, no matter how small, would decorate a float displaying its identity that was pulled along the parade route of Bedford Avenue in the Flatbush section of Brooklyn. Other neighborhoods had their own designated routes.

The vast procession included girls and boys decked out in their Sunday best, Girl Scout and Boy Scout troops, Brownies, Cub Scouts, and all members of Sunday schools no matter what age. Infants and toddlers were pushed in decorated carriages and strollers. The parade represented a diverse array of Brooklyn's humanity, marching to the music each church group assembled. That annual celebration served to both inform and form my identity as a Protestant Christian who would later devote his life to being a professor in Christian education. Christian education was publically celebrated on the streets of Flatbush, Brooklyn every June.

When I was older, I would either wear my white shirt, necktie, and sport jacket while holding the Christian flag or I would wear my scout uniform holding the American flag. This linked service, represented in alternative flag holding, later led to my being awarded the God and Country scout award. In those days, loyalties were aligned with both God and country, with a clear understanding that the United States of America was God's country. My dad had fought in World War II to ensure the world would be safe for all of us. In recognition of his service to others, his name appeared in my local school. On Brooklyn Day, I was proud of my church, my dad, my borough, my country, and my affiliation along with all they represented. That was worth marching for alongside my neighbors. The questions and the critiques of such an alliance laid on the horizon of the sixties.

The flag-holding honors were shared with others when I became old enough to pull or push the church float. Care was required not to move too quickly and run over the marchers in our line. Turning corners required careful coordination with the float team, and if the weather was too hot, I wiped the sweat from my face leaving my sport coat and tie hidden over the float's railing. Being seen as a part of a faithful band from Kenilworth Church and marching in union with other church bands was a spectacle. I looked forward to this event as the end of the school year approached. I have no memories of rain ever canceling the parade's beginning, just one mad rush at the close of one to the church's basement before we could get soaked.

The return to the church, rain or shine, was a highlight because all participants were treated with an unending supply of fruit punch and Italian ice cream cups of chocolate or vanilla with crushed nuts on top. The ice cream was devoured with small wooden spoons in ready supply because some would break on the hard cups stored close to the dry ice in delivery boxes.

The dry ice blocks were themselves objects for grand play. Provided we avoided being burned when extracting them from the boxes, they were placed in the huge church kitchen sinks. After placing them there, we would slowly run the cold water on the blocks creating a wondrous spectacle to behold. The entire church kitchen quickly filled with a thick moist fog that relieved any exhaustion from our parading and even flowed out of the windows over the sinks. Eating ice cream in the fog was a cherished end to each Brooklyn Day.

Lessons Learned

What we are willing to recognize and celebrate in public makes a difference in our sense of identity. The parade route shared with others affirmed the value of gathered faith communities for life's journey.

We are all invited to join a procession through diverse localities, celebrating values and commitments we hold close to our hearts and minds. Adults hope that the patterns of our living and sharing together will shape the characters of children and youth, nurturing a sense of vocation, and supporting the common good, lasting a lifetime. My personal educational journey from boyhood in Brooklyn led to serving as a Christian ambassador in New England these past thirty years and counting.

MY WOODEN CROSS

During my freshman year at Bucknell, my family moved upstairs from our two-bedroom apartment 4G to a three bedroom in 5A. My older sister Laura Lou and I grew up during the lean years of the business, and my brother Ronnie and younger sister Lisa during the fat years. A move from the fourth to sixth floors signaled upward mobility as my dad's process serving business improved. In the move, I lost my small half-sized bedroom, and I felt displaced. It was substituted with the living room sleep sofa as my designated resting place on college vacations. I definitely picked up on the subtle message to move on during or after college. Growing up in our smaller two-bedroom apartment, my three siblings and I regularly negotiated shared living spaces.

With the move, I also lost a small cabinet that housed my childhood treasures, all secured in a red children-sized toolbox. In that box was my rock collection, scout badges, rare coins, camping knives, and objects made at church-related summer camps. The cabinet and box were passed along to Ronnie, seven years my junior. He, in the new apartment, had a large and spacious bedroom all to himself. He needed his own bedroom approaching his teen years.

Upon returning home in June after the move, I was eager to recover my treasures. I found the toolbox with some deep closet digging. But when I opened it, I was astonished to find how little remained. All the neighbors heard my anguished inquiry: "Ronnie, what in the world happened to all of my things! Where are they?"

My mom quickly intervened, and in her presence, Ronnie reluctantly admitted to selling on the corner all that his neighborhood buddies wanted from my precious collection. To add insult to injury, he had also spent all the profits. I could not believe the many things that were now lost—except for a small wooden cross that I had made at Camp Lebanon, New Jersey. I initially felt crucified on that cross in bearing my loss. The loss of treasures signaled a move beyond childhood vestiges.

Later in life, Ronnie worked at stock companies on Wall Street with the business acumen he developed from his street deals. But, many days passed before I could manage to look at Ronnie with any brotherly compassion. To be fair to Ron of today, he did develop a generous heart. Ron readily shares with others in need, not only his brother's treasures, but those of his own. He was recognized, along with his wife Gladys and their son Matthew, by the Reformed Church in America for his service as an elder at a small and struggling New Jersey congregation. Ron and Gladys are pillars in serving their local community. They regularly open their home for shared meals and support of an extended entourage of friends and family. This was a legacy passed on from our parents who practiced the same in all the apartments we occupied on Glenwood Road.

Camp Lebanon is a summer camp of the American Baptist Churches of New Jersey. It was the site of my first sleep-away camp experience at the age of eight. Fortunately, I went along with my older sister and two close older friends from our church, David and Lance Chichester. My parents even treated us with a "black cow" (vanilla ice cream soda made with root beer) at a nearby A&W root beer stand before camp began.

Summer camp was a great adventure in the wilds and farm-lands. An electrical fence divided the platform tent area from the farm field where a huge Black Angus bull was kept. That bull fascinated us the day we arrived. The Chichester brothers and my bunkmates dared me to enter the field, carefully avoiding the electrified fence, to attract the bull with my red windbreaker. As a brash Brooklyn boy, I was up to the challenge. I did manage to get the bull's attention, and was amazed at how fast he approached me from all the way across the wide field. Somehow, by God's grace, I managed to outrun the bull and dive under the fence, impressing my friends with my foolishness.

What I did not manage to avoid (besides the bull) was getting sick four days into the camp week. I tried desperately to hide the soiled underpants I left in the wash house, but I was traced with the obvious name tag my mom had carefully inscribed on all my clothes. I tried to tell my counselor, "Another boy borrowed my pants. I didn't soil these." But he was not convinced and marched me off along with my duffel bag of clothes. The virus I contracted was not to be shared.

Being discovered with a virus meant that I was quarantined in the infirmary for three full camp days. It felt like an eternity los-ing out on all that fun. I missed most the woodworking sessions, where I had started to make a small wooden cross. The project included staining and shellacking. I had managed to cut and attach the three wooden pieces together. I had carefully sanded each of them, but there was no time to complete the job. I felt distraught over not having something special to take home at the end of the week except my underpants.

I pleaded with the nurse, "Please bring the cross here so that I can complete it. I won't make a mess. I promise." But to no avail—her reply each day was "No! You need to get better and rest up."

I didn't come to camp to get rest. "What is wrong with her?" I thought.

I did eventually find things to do at the infirmary. There were books to read, something I tried to avoid during the summer months. The nurse allowed me to work with lanyard (now known as gimp), though it was a favorite of the girls. Other campers were also under quarantine, and we managed to play some card and board games together. But I often thought of my unfinished cross.

The final day of camp arrived and those of us who had recovered from the virus were finally allowed to attend the closing meal and celebration. My bunkmates recounted my run-in with the bull and we all laughed. I had thought about that incident in the infirmary and vowed not to attempt such a stunt again.

At the final camp event in the dining hall, my camp counselor surprised me with the wooden cross I had started, but never finished. I asked him, "Who did this? It looks great." He said, "I did, because you were in the infirmary."

I thanked him with a rare hug and have kept that cross all these years as a keepsake. I have even used it in my own teaching.

Lessons Learned

Life's reversals can provide opportunities for learning. Being dared doesn't mean one should attempt foolish and life-threatening pranks. I learned that bulls could run faster than I could. I also learned that gifts of kindness can last a lifetime in one's memories.

REFLECTIONS ON CHURCH

Kenilworth Baptist Church, located at the pinnacle of the triangular block where Kenilworth and Amersfort Places met Farragut Road, was a white-steepled New England-style edifice that appeared in my Brooklyn neighborhood well before my birth. Given my mom's Baptist roots, my siblings and I attended both Sunday school and church service every week, unless we were sick or out of town. We were decked out in our Sunday best, which for me included a white dress shirt, dark dress pants, laced shoes, and a matching tie. The special attire suggested a serious honoring of God and a commitment to serve others while learning more each week about the Christian faith embraced by our family. That faith was not beyond question however and those questions delayed my expected baptism at the age of thirteen. After the baptismal preparation class led by our pastor, that my older sister and I attended, I opted to wait until my intellectual questions could be addressed. This was a reasoned faith open to critical questions that required careful deliberation before a personal life commitment.

Despite my questions, I faithfully attended church services. My commitment was rewarded with perfect attendance pins every June at the close of the Sunday school year, which corresponded to the end of public school. After the first year's pin, additional years were recognized with attached bars noting the succession of faithful years of attendance. One's accomplished perfect attendance could be celebrated publically when pins were worn for the Brooklyn Day Parade. On these special days, the dangling pin with its attachments was well-secured with pliers prior to the parade to avoid loss.

The weekly commitment to church attendance is a critical issue if church life is to be formative in the lives of both youth and adults. A sustained source for spiritual life requires a routine and ritual for the passage of weeks, seasons and years. Cultural shifts have brought a host of competing activities contending for such loyalties.

In the case of a reasoned faith, the commitment of Jack Cumming, who taught a small class of high school students during Sunday school at Kenilworth, stands out. Jack expected us to write an intelligible paper on a topic from church history. He had us first read the well-written work of Roland H. Bainton entitled *The Church of Our Fathers*, first published in 1941 and dedicated to his children. This work was then copyrighted in 1950 and rededicated to Bainton's grandchildren. Jack wanted us to know our Christian roots and heritage. Today, the title of Bainton's book would more aptly have included both mothers and fathers to honor the key role women have played in the passage of faith across the generations. I then recall writing a paper on Martin Luther, who raised many questions for the church of his time, which provided a rationale for my delayed baptism in order to find some answers worthy of my commitment.

Though my baptism was delayed until 1967, my local church honored my time of searching and questioning. I sang in the choir along with my mom and even taught a kindergarten Sunday school class during my senior year in high school. This may have been penance for the challenges I posed for the series of Sunday school teachers who taught me, but also served to introduce me a life career of teaching related to the Christian church.

5

Agencies/Media

SCOUTS

Brooklyn adventures took on wider circles through my boyhood and youth via scouting programs, all of which met at the Kenilworth Baptist Church, where my family and I regularly attended. The church basement provided an ideal setting for meetings and games like dodgeball, capture the flag, and a host of other fun activities. Here was our alternative to street culture. The walls of this space were ones my dad and I had painted in his service as the ever-faithful church deacon, working on weekends to serve the local flock and our beloved neighborhood. My dad also served as the church representative to the scouting programs. This relationship meant that any transgressions I might commit would be reported to the scouting committee on which my dad sat. It also meant that I performed a caretaker role of sorts in how the scouts used the space that also housed church events. These events included the regular suppers my dad organized as the chief cook, with me as one of his assistants.

My special task at those suppers was to mix the fruit punch served. I delighted in adding just the right mix of canned fruit juices, sherbet, and ginger ale to achieve the puckering of lips by those who imbibed my creative concoctions. No arrow points for cub scouts or merit badges for boy scouts were granted for mixology in those days, but I certainly deserved one.

My dad would often share the expression after enjoying a thirst quenching drink of any kind, "Ah, good beer!" This no doubt was a common utterance from his army service days when, as a technical sergeant, he also did the cooking for his buddies in the Pacific arena during World War II. I knew of the high quality of my non-alcoholic creations when he tasted them and "Ah, good beer!" resounded in the church kitchen. We were not the kind of Baptists who raved against alcohol consumption. We were Brooklyn Baptists.

The other expression my dad often used to provide levity for any occasion, especially with children present, was, "Ebe, sebe, nobo lebe, ebe bamboo!" The best I could tell, these were nonsense words delivered with a Spanish accent that served to provide comic relief to any gathering of church or family. The words reminded us what really was important in gathering with loved ones, like extended and church families, could be enjoyed as nonsense.

Boy Scout overnight outings provided a chance to leave the confines of my beloved Brooklyn and venture into the wilds of Staten Island and upstate New York. Current-day Brooklynites cannot appreciate what travel to these areas via public transportation meant. Before the Verrazano-Narrows Bridge was constructed linking Brooklyn and Staten Island, travel to the ferry meant taking two separate buses, with the requested paper transfer often getting lost in the shuffle, requiring a second fare for unwary scouts. I always secured my paper transfer in a small zippered side compartment of my backpack.

Once on Staten Island, another bus took us to Four Corners where we exited and hiked uphill at least a mile to the William H. Pouch Boy Scout Camp.[1] It was located ever-so-close to the Wil-

---

1. While writing this chapter, I serendipitously learned that two years prior the New York City Council of Scouts had plans to sell Pouch Camp to developers, leading to a public outcry, with scouts and their families demonstrating

lowbrook State Mental Institution. Such a location provided for a memorable first sleep-over initiation that I underwent with the supervision of Scoutmaster Ken. After a year's service, Ken was incidentally relieved of his post by the scout committee.

Ken was a single man in his thirties who sought to teach discipline to the rambunctious city boys of Troop 175, who could usually find humor in any situation. Humorless Ken never ventured a smile, and maintained the demeanor of a rugged outdoors adventurer, running a tight ship in all aspects of life, including his troops, under his strong and direct leadership.

Ken expected immediate obedience to all his commands during the overnight hike. Failure resulted in corporal punishment that included a Sisyphean task. A big rock was found and tossed in a muddy stream and placed at the bottom of a high hill. The offending scout would then be required to push that heavy rock up the hill as penance for his offense. I cannot recall what particular offense resulted in Ken's wrath in my case, but I think everyone had their turn with this punishment of mythological proportions. I do recall my raw hands after my turn on the hill and careful listening for all subsequent instructions barked by Ken to his oppressed underlings.

After an exhausting day of traveling, hiking, setting up camp, preparing meals, and meticulous clean-up, the troop gathered around the campfire for a hair-raising horror story shared by Ken.

"You boys have seen the mental institution, Willowbrook, that we passed on our hike up here from Four Corners."

We all nodded.

"What I did not tell you is that an alert was shared that one of their patients has just escaped. A patient by the name of Lisa."

"Oh, no, just what I don't need," I thought to myself.

"Lisa lived a very hard life in the woods close by Pouch Camp. Her husband abused her and left soon after her beloved son was

---

to find a way to prevent the sale. Given their response, the New York Times reported on July 7, 2011, that a plan had been developed to save the camp by a deal the Boy Scouts of America had secured with The Trust for Public Land. This urban oasis, that had made a difference in many scouts' lives, was safe.

born. She eked out a living by gathering plants from the very woods we have hiked through today."

"One fateful day, while gathering berries near where we are sleeping tonight, a terrible accident occurred. Lisa and her young son Johnny were behind some bushes while a careless boy scout was nearby playing with his new sharpened axe."

"The scout heard a noise in the bush and thought it was a raccoon that was stealing his troop's food. He foolishly threw his axe right into the bush and tragically killed Lisa's beloved son right before her eyes."

"Lisa went wild and picked up the axe from her son's split head and ran after that boy scout and all his friends. But, before she could kill him, she fell and was restrained by the camp director, who just happened to be nearby on his regular rounds."

"Lisa went insane and was committed to live the rest of her life in the nearby mental institution. But, be warned, that she vowed if she ever escaped, she would kill every scout in her sight as a payment for the tragedy that befell her beloved Johnny."

"I want you all to rest tonight, but, if you hear any sounds of an axe cutting wood late tonight, it may well be Lisa seeking her revenge on us. So keep alert, even in your sleep!"

As might be imagined, we were wakened in the middle of the night by an axe chopping at the rear of our wooden lean-to enclosure. Frightened out of my wits, I ran for my life and was only deterred slightly by shouts from my comrades, "Watch out for the creek! Jump!"

I barely saw the approaching creek and jumped as far as I could to avoid the water. I fell in a heap on the other side and only breathed a sigh of relief when I heard the laughter and assurances of Ken and the senior scouts who were clearly in the know.

"Stop running! It was just a part of your initiation. There is no Lisa!"

"Hey, Paz, look! [Paz was my nickname] Wow, quite a jump! It was about twenty feet. How did you do that?"

"I was so afraid and didn't want to die! I really believed that story," as my heart was still racing.

Once back at home, and thoroughly exhausted from my first overnight with little sleep, I was surprised by family news: that very weekend my mom had given birth to a new sibling, a girl. I asked my older sister Laura Lou about her name. To my shock and dismay she said: "Lisa Ann."

"Oh no! Oh no! Not Lisa!"

After stories of Ken's usual tactics eventually filtered to the scouting committee, the troop soon learned that a new scoutmaster had been appointed. His name was Bernie. Compared to stern Ken, Bernie was a jovial, fun-loving, and huge man, who just happened to have a bakery delivery service with a van that could accommodate us on travel to Boy Scout camps. To our amazement and delight, the truck also carried every kind of excess baked goods that we could consume on our weekends away in the woods. Sweet tooth heaven was ours, in addition to time away from home! What more could be asked for? My dental records confirm these excesses.

Given that Bernie worked all night, he needed his sleep on our weekends together. Therefore, Bernie's tent was off limits to any uptight camp officials who dared to complain about the antics of Troop 175's members who warranted immediate camp expulsion.

Bernie was a bear of a man and signaled his deep sleep with loud snores. When awakened before the appointed afternoon hour of about 3:00 pm on Saturdays, Bernie was not a happy person and was known to toss folks out of his tent for disturbing his well-deserved sleep.

Out from under Ken's watchful eye, Troop 175 adopted the new nickname of "the whoopee tribe," as we tested limits with a host of clever antics. At one camp, we went into the lake and used rowboats at an unappointed hour. This travesty resulted in the camp director's demand for a visit with our Scoutmaster Bernie. We informed the director and his trusty assistants that Bernie would be in his tent at 10:00 am sharp and they could go in and speak directly to him then. These were his clear orders, and we were obedient scouts.

At 9:30 am, we strategically placed a large surplus can of Heinz baked beans in the campfire located just outside of Bernie's tent. As well-trained and cautious scouts, we all gathered at a safe distance. A second can was placed in the fire at 9:32 am. Through numerous careful experiments with just the right size fire and positioning of the cans, we determined with amazing accuracy when the cans would blow and in what direction. After all, surplus beans were expendable given all the cakes and cookies we had to eat.

At 10:00 am, the irate camp director arrived right to our campsite and demanded to see our scoutmaster—right on time. He was slight in build and impeccably dressed in scouting attire, with a wide-brimmed campaign hat and numerous patches carefully sewn on his pressed uniform.

"Bernie is sleeping right in that tent, but he told us to wake him up at any time if he was really needed. Go on in."

"It sure is needed in your case!" the director barked.

We heard Bernie's snoring cease and waited with delight to see the camp director fly out of the tent with Bernie's able assistance. Within a few seconds the first bean can blew and coated the camp director from head to toe in delicious Heinz baked beans, though they smelled a bit burnt. Just as he stood up and his trusty assistants rushed to his aid, the second can blew. All three were thoroughly coated.

We heard them say in their rapid retreat, "Well, I have never been treated like this. It is shameful! Troop 175 will surely be banned from this camp!"

"Oh well, we'll just have to try another camp next month" we thought.

But, he could have responded: "Ah, good beans!"

After the director stamped off defeated from the antics at our campsite, we heard Bernie's inquiry: "What is going on out there?"

"Nothing, Bernie. Just go back to sleep. We know you need your rest!"

And that is exactly what he did.

Lessons Learned

From scoutmasters Ken and Bernie I learned the difference between autocratic and laissez-faire leadership. With Ken, I discovered that leadership can take different forms and be used to scare the wits out of any initiates through fear. With Bernie, I discovered the value of freedom in exploring responsibility with those under one's supervision. Each leader presented his challenges, though we preferred our freedom and creativity under Bernie. Boy Scouts intended to build character and, in the process, included among its ranks a number of fascinating characters. One of those characters included me, as I passed through the ranks of tenderfoot, second-class, and first-class scout. The earning of merit badges was definitely frowned upon by me and my buddies in Troop 175, who just wanted to have a fun time wherever we went, often to outrageous extremes. (If the Little Rascals from television were our age and could have joined the scouts, they would have felt right at home.) Therefore, I never progressed to become an eagle scout, which most other troops encouraged. Troop 175 was the "whoopee tribe," and the call that went up from any scout at all-district or city-wide jamborees was "Whoo, whoo." Our orchestrated response was "Whoopee," to the great consternation of scout officials. This also incited rivalry with other troops, whom I think envied our glorious freedom and spontaneity under Bernie's loveable leadership.

To Ken's credit, when we visited Pouch Camp, he did ask for volunteers to attend the local Moravian Church located close by for Sunday service. I was one of the few who accompanied him. Later in my scout career, I received the God and Country award, for which I was gifted with an actual medal to wear on my uniform. I also eventually became patrol leader and senior patrol leader. That led to my induction in the Order of the Arrow, a secret scout unit that required a silent initiation work ordeal and provided a sash emblazoned with a red arrow—another noteworthy uniform addition.

The scout motto of "be prepared" has characterized my professional life with folks commenting over the years about my organizational skills. Under Ken and Bernie, I had to be prepared for anything and care for those under my watch. The legacy of Troop 175 continues in my looking for the fun in any life situation, calling for creative impishness when needed to foster group morale.

Lessons Applied

Leadership assumed a different character when I was appointed the Senior Patrol Leader of Troop 175. I was called upon to provide oversight and care for a ragtag troop that delighted in being mischievous at every opportunity. One incident that stands out was the challenge of leaving Pouch Camp on Staten Island after our ban was lifted in time to make the Brooklyn ferry connection going back home.

Stevie was the assistant scoutmaster who accompanied us when Bernie could not attend. But Stevie was a young adult with definite mental disabilities. During this particular weekend, Stevie had frequent clashes with Mike Berg, an angry and sadistic older scout who was also a patrol leader. Just before departing the Pouch PX and hiking down to the bus stop en route to the ferry, Stevie had a special request for me.

"Bobby, I need to buy my ice cream sandwich before I go. I can't leave without my ice cream. I need it."

Mike threatened, "Stevie, if you make us late for the ferry, I am going to cut you up with my knife," brandishing the razor-sharp blade for all to see.

My quick response was "Stop it both of you! Mike, put the knife away. Stevie, go quickly and buy your ice cream sandwich, but we have to start and you will just have to catch up."

"No, Bobby, no, wait for me! You have to wait!"

"No, Stevie, we have to get started to make the boat. You can run to catch up after you get your ice cream. Give me your backpack to carry."

Somehow we all made it to the ferry despite the theatrics with the ice cream sandwich and no knife cuts were sustained.

Leadership often requires confrontation and clear directions under duress, choosing the best options available at the time while avoiding disaster.

TELEVISION

Television did not enter my home until I was seven years old. My dad, who liked to fiddle with his hands when he was not cooking, put together a television screen with all its tubes on one table, using the adjacent table for the speaker. Being a visual learner, I always focused on the screen, but an auditory learner may have been distracted with such a disjointed media presentation. I became aware of my preferred visual learning style from any early age.

The television shows I most enjoyed watching, apart from sporting events (such as the Dodgers games), were late-night horror movies we watched together as a family, which we accompanied with pizza. The pizza consisted of thick-crusted rectangular Sicilian style purchased at the Pizza Den on Flatbush Avenue. We all sprawled out across my parents' sofa bed in our living room. After my younger siblings arrived and my older sister and I had entered adolescence, we needed our own space. My parents sacrificed their bedroom, dividing it in half with a wall to allow Laura Lou and I to have our own narrow rooms. The limited space we each had was good preparation for college dorms we later occupied. Ronnie, my brother, and Lisa shared the other bedroom with their bunk beds.

Watching Count Dracula suck the blood of his victims was accompanied by my licking and sucking the red pizza sauce. These antics promoted cries and screams from my siblings.

"Mom, Bobby is being gross again, he's scaring us!"

My protest in reply was, "It tastes so good and I want to suck your blood!," as I imitated Lon Chaney and a Transylvanian accent.

We would all laugh and check to see how many pieces of pizza remained to fuel my best impression.

If the protesting of my siblings became loud enough to prevent listening of the film, my dad would voice, "Basta! Basta!" In

Spanish *basta* means "enough" and I knew I had reached my theatrical limit.

I do recall the typical children's shows that my peers still remember: *Flash Gordon, Hop-Along Cassidy, Superman, The Lone Ranger, The Cisco Kid* and *Captain Midnight,* although I always preferred to be outside playing rather than in the apartment. My older sister also had first dibs on what we watched and she loved the repeated showings of *The Million Dollar Movie* so much so that she was eventually able to memorize most of the actors' lines.

Apart from television, newspapers were available every day at home. On the subway to Manhattan my dad would read the *New York Times* and the *Daily News* to check baseball scores. These were available to use upon his return each weekday night. On the weekend I was sent to purchase the papers at one of the local candy stores along with some of my favorite sweets depending on my available cash. Radio listening was a challenge with younger siblings who always loved to play games.

Our favorite game involved water guns, with which we managed to soak most of the apartment walls. Once, when we graduated to actual buckets of water and my mom was out, our downstairs neighbor protested the leaks that had suddenly begun to stream down her walls. Our other daring water sport involved balloons filled with care and tossed from our fourth-floor window onto unsuspecting pedestrians.

The water balloon toss eventually progressed to the feat of filling a five-foot long multicolored heavyweight balloon that was carefully carried to the roof of our six-story building with my buddies, John Reily and Scott Drake. From that height, the balloon was dropped onto the sidewalk. Thank God no one was killed with that reckless behavior, and we eventfully thought better of a repeat effort. I can just imagine a *Daily News* headline reading: "Unwary Pedestrian Killed by Children's Water Balloon."

LESSONS LEARNED

Media via the television and films provided entertainment and an escape from daily routines. Viewing with family and friends provided a shared experience but minimal imaginative exploration as compared with reading and play. The one exception was *The Little Rascals* because it nurtured antics we explored in the scouts.

REFLECTIONS ON AGENCIES AND MEDIA

I link together social agencies and media because they both serve to provide windows into the larger society. They also affirm development of children and youth with that world. This was the case for me.

Through the scouting programs that met at my local church, my social, emotional and leadership development was fostered. My skills were tested and affirmed in relationships to peers and explored in the interplay of articulated ideals for shared life and adventure. Achievements were recognized and specifically related to others' advancements as we ventured into camp settings to explore nature and our own identities. The wonder of the woods, a relatively short distance from city sidewalks and endless pavements, fascinated as well as terrorized scouts, as did the stories of wild things and people in close proximity in the woods. Venturing into the unknown was less fearful when accompanied by others like myself and effectively guided by those with more experience. Outside the safety of home, new skills were engaged for survival.

On one trip to Pouch Camp, when one scout set off some firecrackers, a forest fire broke out due to dry fall conditions. The danger called for all scouts to help and assistance of other troops nearby was called upon to avert a real disaster of our own making. Fortunately, proper techniques were recalled and the fire extinguished without injury. Much was learned from the near tragedy about what not to do, despite my earlier warnings as patrol leader about the firecrackers being a potential problem.

The media's impact had a more limited influence during my upbringing as compared with its current dominance in the lives of children and youth. Television, radio and newspapers were ever present, but the clear preference was to play outdoors among peers who also lived in cramped spaces. The one home resource I readily used was the Encyclopedia Britannica that my mom had purchased with her household savings from a salesman who came to our door. The encyclopedia fueled my academic interest right at home to complement visits to the New York Public Library branch located on Nostrand Avenue between Glenwood and Farragut Roads.

The entertainment value of films and televised sporting events was valued as shared family time. In the case of late-night horror films, viewing provided the opportunity to enjoy pizza which was often used to imitate the blood sucking adventures of a vampire like Béla Lugosi, or roles played by Boris Karloff and Lon Chaney as Frankenstein, the mummy or wolf man. Family board games and reading provided more treasured times as compared with media viewing except for visits to movie theatres shared with peers during my teen years.

6

Economy

EARNING MONEY

My older sister Laura Lou and I grew up during the lean years of our dad's Paragon Process Serving business. He was too kind-hearted, almost to a fault. He did not demand much from his employees, who would have found it difficult obtaining employment elsewhere. Those employees demonstrated loyalty and great appreciation anytime we visited the Paragon offices or when they visited our home. By comparison, my younger brother by seven years, Ronnie, and younger sister, Lisa, by eleven years grew up during the fat or prosperous years of dad's business. To this day, frugality characterizes the lives of Laura Lou and me, and relative extravagance in the case of Ron and Lisa. Laura Lou, still laughs about our difference with younger siblings.

Given the lean years, Laura Lou and I always valued the habits of saving money, as exemplified by my mother. I recall our monthly visits to the impressive Flatbush Savings Bank located near the junction of Flatbush and Nostrand Avenues. A bank guard was present at the front entrance, and bronze metal railings separated the tellers from those doing business. I possessed a blue savings account booklet that tabulated all my hard-earned deposits with few withdrawals noted because I was saving for college and spent as little of my allowance as possible except for regular visits to the candy stores for my favorite treats. My favorites were strawberry licorice and chunky bars that contained raisins and nuts in a thick chocolate cube on which I nibbled to last a long time.

I remember that rent day was the fifteenth of every month, as my birthday just happened to fall on June fifteenth. Birthday celebrations during my early years were sparse, but what I did receive was greatly treasured, as it represented a sacrifice in light of a tight family budget. My first two-wheel bike was second-hand, but my dad had spent time in secret at the home of the Chichester family carefully painting it. The stripes on the bike were black, red, silver and white, unlike those of any of my playmates, and easily identifiable.

Another memorable gift that awaited a Christmas celebration was a radio construction kit that necessitated precious evening times with dad to put together. The exterior of the radio was silver with large black dials to control the power, tuning and volume. All the radio tubes gave off amber lights and could be seen from the brown perforated back panel when in operation.

I had seen my dad construct our first television with a speaker separated from the picture tube until we could later afford a manufactured set. With the older homemade set, when a tube would blow, I accompanied my dad to the local electronics store with a bag full of tubes that were possible suspects, where a convenient tube-tester helped us to discover the real culprit. With our new tube replacement, we rushed home to complete the repair and again view favorite programs like *The Lone Ranger, The Cisco Kid, Buck Rogers, Captain Midnight,* or late-night horror movies often accompanied by rectangular pizza fresh from The Pizza Den up on Flatbush Avenue.

The delight of repairing and mending broken home items continues for me to this day in lieu of the more common consumer option of rapid replacement. Just think of all the money saved! After all, a Boy Scout is "thrifty," as I recited—along with "trustworthy, loyal, helpful, friendly, courteous, kind, obedient, cheerful, thrifty brave, clean and reverent"—in my cherished Boy Scout Law.

As a result of our tight family budget, I do recall placing less-valued baseball cards in the bottom of my sneakers to cover the holes and thereby avoid additional holes in my socks that would have to be sewn carefully to avoid the bumps that eventually caused blisters from playing. With all of the hard ball-playing on side-walks and city streets, even Converse sneakers took such a beating, but replacements were expensive and too often required. Sneakers from Thom McAn shoe store were less expensive, but also not as sturdy as Converse. Because they wore out quicker they required more cards to cover the holes I managed to readily produce with my love of running.

Given my boyhood financial challenges, earning money was a priority. With four children still at home, weekly allowances were sparse. While I began earning money by helping out my neighbor Reddy once a week, a steadier income was needed. Bobby Robinson, who lived on the other and economically better side of Bedford Avenue, was my ticket. Bobby and I were in Cub Scouts together and we soon became friends as high achievers. Bobby lived in a private home with his mom, a school principal, and his dad, a dentist. Bobby's neighbors had a number of chores just right for energetic boys wanting to earn extra spending money.

The one particular job etched in my memory was secured from Dr. Shebelle's wife. Dr. Shebelle was our family physician and he lived and practiced medicine just down the block from the Robinsons on East 21st Street. He was a short and thin man, soft-spoken and typically attired in a dark three-piece suit under his white jacket. He reminded me of photos of my great grandfather Felicísimo López, who was also a doctor. His wire-rimmed glasses often sat low on his nose as he gently examined whatever ailing portion of my body required his special care. Dr. Shebelle was well-respected in my family because he had miraculously sown together the palm of my dad's hand after a freak accident just before Sunday worship that involved changing a tire.

Before he came to an active faith, my dad would always drive folks to church on Sunday mornings. But, on that fateful morning, he discovered a flat tire that required a quick change so as not to disappoint awaiting churchgoers. In the rush to replace the tire, the jack was not securely stationed under the car. When the car was jacked up high and awaiting an inflated spare, the jack began to slip and tilt over. My dad's first response was to grab the car just under the wheel well to prevent a break in the now-exposed axle. The family budget only allowed the purchase of used cars, and each one had to last a long time. The metal was too sharp and opened a wide gash in my dad's right hand. Blood was everywhere. As I watched these events half in shock and disbelief, my dad wrapped a towel around his wound and called up to mom, who soon appeared from our fourth floor apartment window.

"Laura, I need to see a doctor. I cut my hand!"

She responded, "Get to Dr. Shebelle! I'll call him."

A neighbor who heard the exchange volunteered to drive and off my dad went. My mom called those stranded awaiting a ride and the church office.

Mom instructed us: "Go on to church and ask for prayers for your dad!"

I did see my dad after church all bandaged up and grateful for the care he received. Over the years he always would hold out his right hand when recounting the amazing healing of a body part used so often in preparing church suppers and completing numerous jobs around the church property. Hands were also used to serve and welcome others, a fact just as we sang in Sunday school:

> Be careful little hands what you do,
> be careful little hands what you do.
> There's a Father up above and He is looking down in love,
> So be careful little hands what you do.

Hands were used to earn money, and Bobby and I hired out ours to assist our new employer, Mrs. Shebelle. By comparison with her husband, she was a huge-framed, stocky woman with a stern demeanor. Her dark black hair speckled with gray was affixed in a tight bun held in place with a turtle-shell barrette. That day she wore a fine blue-and-white printed, floral dress covered by a well-worn apron with numerous pockets. She had to easily weigh twice her husband.

When we arrived at the arranged time of eight o'clock at her back porch, she nodded and said, "Your job today, boys, is to dig out every dandelion weed from my lawn," as she peered across a huge expanse of green pocketed with yellow flowers, too many to count. She handed us each long garden pokers and warned: "You'll be paid five cents for each dandelion, but only if you show me the whole dandelion including its roots. And you must clear the entire lawn of dandelions before you will get paid. No exceptions."

Her bedside manner was nothing like her husband's as indicated by her scowl and warning to us, "I will be watching you!" True to her word, she did periodically peer out of her kitchen window to check on our progress.

The idea of five cents per dandelion motivated great energy as I anticipated each candy bar purchase that could be made per weed extraction. Lawn work took concentration on a hot and humid summer day with few breezes. As the day wore on, I asked my friend, "Bobby, will we ever finish this? Boy is she that mean, not to pay us if we don't finish today? That is not fair."

I was relieved when Mrs. Shebelle showed up at noon with lunch for us, which included peanut butter and jelly sandwiches and large, colored aluminum glasses full of refreshing fruit juice. She shared her mid-day report on our progress: "You are doing well and I hope you keep up the good work." Bobby smiled when she disappeared back into her kitchen explaining, "Her bark is worse than her bite." He had worked for her before on a solo basis, but this job required the handy-boy team we had organized.

With renewed spirits, we returned to our task. We were surprised again with an afternoon snack of cookies and cold ice water in those aluminum glasses that helped soothe our hands, which were sore from this hard manual labor. My fingers ached from all that digging and extraction of roots. I would certainly need to scrub my nails with the brush at home to clean up.

Our job was completed around three o'clock and we waited at the back steps for the final accounting of the wicker buckets chock-full of dandelions. This time, Mrs. Shebelle greeted us with half a smile. She surveyed the lawn, now completely green with no yellow intruders to be seen.

"Let's see how many dandelions we have here," as she carefully examined each plant for intact roots. Ones with full roots were piled to the right side, and those without on the left. My fear was that nothing would be paid for those on the left.

"I will pay you five cents for every two of those on the left," she graciously noted to my great surprise.

In the end, I was relieved. Bobby and I had a handsome wage for the tedious but rewarding day of dandelion extraction at the Shebelle house.

Lessons Learned

Hard work could be rewarded with a fair employer. Working on a team makes a difference in completing tasks. Being industrious can be motivational even when playing ball was more attractive on a bright summer day. Beyond the work to earn money was the work in serving others. Serving on the AAA crossing guard squad at P. S. 152 and later on the audio-visual and social studies textbook squad with George Marmorino at Andries Hudde, I learned the importance of serving others well. Such lessons reinforced what my parents modeled for us in our home, neighborhood, and local church about caring for others in need and expressing in action the love we sang about in worship each week. The attitude, fairness, and care of one's employer certainly make a difference in how any work may progress.

DAD'S BUSINESS AND LORD'S BAKERY

At the intersection of Flatbush and Nostrand Avenues, a host of stores could be found to meet most shopping needs for our day-to-day life. "The junction," as it was known, was at the last spot of the IRT (Interborough Rapid Transit) Flatbush subway line, which connected Brooklyn with the city. Though, officially Brooklyn was a borough of New York City, we referred to Manhattan as "the city." Brooklyn was, in many ways, its own world, separate from the city center of national and international business, cultural, political, and educational life, all found on the island of Manhattan.

We learned at P. S. 152 that Manhattan had been purchased from the naïve Native Americans by the Dutch colonists for only $24.00. "What a bargain!" Those early Dutch colonists must have been thrifty as I was taught in scouts, or, on second thought, "Were the colonists scalping the natives?" Most likely it was the second scenario, from what I knew of street life. I too was thrifty like my Dutch forebears.

The Flatbush IRT stop was where my dad entered and emerged each day from business life at his 261 Broadway office. My dad was a partner in the Paragon Process Serving business, which served the legal and court systems by distributing of subpoenas and summons to appear and serve as a witness in various state and federal courts. His partner was Frank O'Connell, who managed billing and the financial side of the business, while my dad interfaced with the clients, employees, and process servers in the serving of legal papers.

Prior to military service my dad worked as a court clerk, which required careful listening and recording of court procedures. His preference was to be his own boss; this meant that my older sister Laura Lou and I grew up during the lean years when the business was starting up, while my younger brother by seven years, Ron, and younger sister by eleven years, Lisa, grew up during the fat years. As you might imagine, Laura Lou and I are known for our frugality in household economics, whereas Ron and Lisa are known for their generous and easy-spending ways. In some ways, this was a tale of two different families on the economic front given the large age span between the siblings replicated in my own immediate family with a twelve-year age span between our two children.

Differences in economic perspective were also operative in the division of household labor. On the home front, my dad's primary business was food purchase and preparation during the big weekend meals that often had guests in attendance. One of my weekly joys was accompanying him for food shopping on early Saturday mornings and frequenting all the stores that sold their specialties. My mom's housework included all the cleaning and co-ordination of schedules centered on the care of children. My older sister and I helped in these areas and both eventually explored careers in education. But shopping on the weekends assisting my dad and shopping for any weekday needs was my domain, which required acquaintance with the neighborhood stores.

Lord's Bakery was one of those junction businesses an easy stop off of the subway on my dad's way home. It was just a short three-block walk from our apartment if I was sent to make purchases. All the offerings from this Jewish bakery were beautifully displayed in the front window, tempting the attention of any pass-ersby. Upon entering the store a customer pressed a beige metal dispenser to receive a purple ticket marked with a number dictating the order of individual. In turn, each clerk tugged on a metal chain attached to a large rectangular black counter to display the next customer number in white, while calling the number out loudly in the hopes that the person with that number on his/her ticket would hear. Calling out loud was required because many customers, like me, were mesmerized with all the sugar-laden de-lights that filled the glass display shelves to the brim. My favorites were the cookies and rugelach, a rolled pastry filled with nuts, raisins, chocolate bits or raspberry and dipped in honey or sugar and cinnamon. These latter treats would melt in your mouth and provide enough bites to savor the mix of flavors over an extended period of time. Each bite was often accompanied by the closing of one's eyes to extract the height of culinary bliss. In this way, the soul was fed along with one's sweet tooth.

During the lean years, not many stops at Lord's were possible on my dad's trip home. But, during the fat years the cardboard boxes bound tightly with multiple strands of red and white striped string more readily appeared, filled with pastries carefully wrapped in translucent tissue paper to keep them safe on the walk home. The boxes were tied so tight that only a whiff could be extracted before arriving home, and the knots so wound that only a scissor or knife could be used to release the treasures within. Patience was expected and the Lord's boxes were usually opened only after the meal in time for dessert.

I can still hear my parents' response to requests for just one taste: "We are all waiting until after the meal before we can enjoy the sweets."

Being a food grazer, I felt challenged after having smelled the delights emanating from the corners of the box. But I was always the ready volunteer to help clear the table after meals to speed up the long-awaited dessert presentation.

Lessons Learned

Being in a family of foodies meant that love and care for others was closely associated with shared meals. When our family budget allowed, the additional treats from Lord's Bakery added delights for all and a complement to the sustenance we all needed. Relationships are strengthened through shared meals and strangers readily become new friends in the mix.

REFLECTIONS ON ECONOMY

The economy was explored through the work of caring for and repairing the world using our God-given gifts. In the case of my father, this was modeled both in the lean and fat years of his legal serving business. My father's clients were lawyers and the companies they served. During the lean years, those clients proved to be unreliable in making payments for the services they received. My father's partner, who struggled with alcoholism and was responsible for the billing and tax payments, also proved to be unreliable. In the midst of those challenges, my father demonstrated a commitment to people that went beyond bottom-line financial concerns. Some of his employees were less than stellar in their performance, but his commitment to them meant an unfortunate reluctance to confront those issues. By comparison, I have sought to combine both commitments to individuals and the tasks at hand in my work and leadership. This has involved a willingness to raise key questions and issues in difficult situations that others would prefer not to raise. Caring enough to confront others does come with its costs, but it can also serve a business or a group in the long run.

My mother's industrious spirit was modeled when she was unable to work outside of the home with four children under her care. After working as a dental assistant on weekends during part of my childhood, she pursued home-based businesses like Avon, Nutrilite, and Nature's Sunshine. She also helped with the clerical work required as part of my father's business by periodically performing typing tasks at home. I do recall that her hospitalizations for ulcers, perhaps related to our financial struggles, called for the household management skills of both my older sister Laura Lou and me. With siblings seven and eleven years younger than me, we were inducted into service developing our culinary and cleaning abilities in the process of maintaining a household.

Work was directly related to serving others in our home. Work also involved serving in the church as described earlier and caring for our neighbors like Reddy and working for Mrs. Shebelle. Homework or housework was honored and required the best efforts of all family members doing their parts, with egalitarian commitments modeled by my parents. Both my father and mother cooked. Dad cooked on weekends and mom during the week. Both my parents worked inside and outside our home to support and enrich our family and neighbors. All hands were required for cleaning, and shopping was the domain of my father, the provider, assisted by me and then later by one of my siblings when I left for college. Work was an avenue to earn money and care for others.

7

Body Politic

POLITICAL PARTIES

My childhood awareness of political issues and alliances came from observing the regular voting habits of my parents at the local polling location housed in P. S. 152, my elementary school. I observed the mysterious booths stationed in the school's basement where adults checked in and disappeared behind the curtains to record their vote. Newspaper articles named the candidates, and issues and television news reports informed us of rallies being held and results of elections. With divisive political races, a wealth of buttons appeared, displaying the faces of candidates fixed for attention. One large campaign button I remember had General Eisenhower's face with "I Like Ike" emblazoned in bold along the border.

My mom's political leanings were clear: "We are Republicans because they support small businessmen just like your dad." She echoed the sentiments of her family of origin in Pennsylvania. "Republicans support the army and your dad served in the army during World War II!"

I was less sure about my dad's political leanings because they were never a part of our family discussions. But, based on my mom's perspective, I thought he likely shared her Republican leanings.

The sense of this family Republican affiliation was only tested once I entered junior high school and the hotly contested 1960 presidential election pitted Richard Nixon against John Kennedy. My dynamic social studies teacher, Ms. Bragan, proposed a classroom debate between Nixon and Kennedy supporters. Ms. Bragan was beautiful and I very much wanted to please and impress her, so I volunteered to argue in class for Nixon, along with my newfound buddy, George Marmorino, against two young women from class who supported Kennedy. After the debate, our class voted and, to our surprise, Kennedy won. I did have to admit that John Kennedy was the more attractive candidate, even if he was Catholic. The country agreed with the class in that momentous vote and I began to question the views I supported during our class' debate.

The ideals President Kennedy advocated stirred my feelings as we began to study the legacy of ancient Greeks and Romans in the junior high social studies curriculum. George and I were so stirred that we bought a black, hard, rubber practice-discus and practiced throwing it in the fields of Brooklyn College and the sands of Riis Park beach, reliving the glory of ancient times. Our imaginations were nurtured by the Hercules movies playing in local theaters, displaying the finely sculptured body of Steve Reeves. As our bodies matured, here was an ideal worth striving towards given our increased interest in attracting classmates of the opposite sex.

George's dad was Italian and his mom was Puerto Rican. With my Ecuadorean dad and Dutch and German mom, we shared a similar ethnic mix. He was Methodist and I was a Baptist, so we shared religious backgrounds as Protestants. His three older sisters were athletes who competed nationally and their accomplishments were a motivation for our common athletic interests. George and I were both good runners and we wanted to do well academically and in sports, embracing the best of both Sparta and Athens. The ideals of scholastic and athletic competition enthralled us. The world was opened up before us as we read Shakespeare's *Romeo and Juliet*. The love of life, the longed-for love of young women, and the love of study were intoxicating, as we fully embraced the three-year special education program that was reserved for gifted junior high students like ourselves.

What confounded us were the increasingly troubling political and social realities that unfolded during the sixties. Our ideals confronted those shifting realities and divided alliances beyond adolescent hopes for a better world and our place in it. My junior and senior high years along with college filled the decade from 1960 to 1970; I graduated from Bucknell University in May 1970. My last semester at Bucknell was curtailed by an all-campus student strike in protest of the Vietnam War. By that time, I had been married for nine months and received news that my wife was pregnant. I had a low draft number as far as Brooklyn recruits went, and was headed back to New York City without a job and with a psychology major in hand that was not promising lucrative, if any, employment. How would my ideals play out in a politically confused nation and world?

I had survived the sixties, but what was my future with a child on the way and no solid job prospects in sight? I recalled the line from Laurel and Hardy comedies, "This is another fine mess you have gotten us into!" Blame could not be affixed on anyone else, but myself.

Lessons Learned

Conscious political realities emerged slowly in my life as national, local, and global issues dominated the media. The assassinations of John Kennedy, Robert Kennedy, and Martin Luther King Jr. brought harsh challenges to the ideals I had embraced in school in concert with my family and church. What was possible in terms of justice and equity when violence loomed around the corner? How could one's life make a difference in a world of increasing change and dislocation? My political leanings were more associated with the Democratic Party as compared with my parents' Republican leanings.

REFLECTIONS ON BODY POLITIC

Consciousness of the political realities of my world began to emerge when I entered junior high school during the 1960 election of John F. Kennedy. During those years, the social studies of cultures and societies provided perspective on the wider society in which I was enmeshed. The turbulent sixties introduced alternatives for the United States from inherited patterns and raised questions not easily answered about current power dynamics. While intellectually exploring new areas in my earlier adolescent years, my social and emotional development was more engaged with youth issues than national and global concerns.

My later formation of ideals confronted the increasing harsh realities of a troubled nation and world. During my earlier adolescence, my safe response was to embrace the espoused political leanings of my parents. Serious political engagement awaited my college years and my coming of voting age. The Bucknell campus provided the setting in which to explore the state of the nation and world with new questions and lenses. The epilogue recounts this part of my life journey.

Epilogue

A Brooklyn Baptist Boy Goes to Bucknell

The title to this epilogue did not appear as a headline in the *New York Times*, the *Daily News*, the *New York Post*, or even the *Brooklyn Eagle*. Nevertheless, such a headline captures my transition from boyhood to the adult world in 1966. After all, I was eighteen and leaving Brooklyn for central Pennsylvania and the small town of Lewisburg. Coming from the city, I fell in love with the campus setting when I first visited it in May 1966.

Being a Baptist from Brooklyn who went to Bucknell became significant twenty years later in 1986 when I joined the faculty of Andover Newton Theological School where two other members remarkably shared this very same heritage. Both Gabriel Fackre, who taught theology, and George H. Sinclair, Jr., who taught church administration, shared these roots and their arrival predated mine. The formative influences of our Brooklyn setting and the impact of local churches for life trajectories are noteworthy for each of us. Gabe came from Lebanese heritage and George from Scottish roots, but we all shared the welcome Brooklyn offered to generations of immigrant peoples entering the main stream of American life.

Whereas Bucknell had Baptist roots, in 1966 it was a non-sectarian school that welcomed study in a wide variety of areas including geology, religion, and eventually psychology, which drew my interest. It was well known for its strong fraternity and sorority life, which I briefly explored but opted instead for independent associations that centered upon the Christian community and fellowship on and off campus in Lewisburg.

Upon arriving at Bucknell for my freshman year I was directly confronted with class differences not noted in college catalogues. My roommate Brian had attended an elite private prep school and was recruited for the swim team. He was tall, broad-shouldered, and oozed confidence regarding his privileged place on campus.

I had arrived first to our shared dorm room on the second floor of Trax Hall and had placed my two blazers, shirts, and pants in one of the closets, taking up only one-third of my allotted space. Brian arrived with such a huge wardrobe that his closet quickly filled, with many clothes left in piles upon his bed. The number of suits he brought alone astounded me. I graciously offered: "Brian, please go ahead and use the remaining space in my closet. I for sure will not need it the rest of the year."

I had been driven to college accompanied only by my dad, who also had to drive my sister back to her third year at Potsdam State College in upstate New York, which was an eight-hour drive each way. The trip to Lewisburg was too long for my mom and younger siblings to take before Interstate 80 was completed from New York. My dad and I had traveled on state route 46 through too many New Jersey towns. He had to rush right back to Brooklyn with few resources even to consider staying the night.

Brian arrived with his entire family including siblings in tow with plans to stay nearby in launching Brian. His parents' first question for me was:

"Robert, please tell us where did you attend high school?"

It was followed by: "Is Midwood a private or public school?"

"Aren't your parents here and staying for the weekend?"

Their questions put me in my place in the college social scene. I sensed that I was well beyond my league in choosing to attend

Bucknell. I thought that Princeton and Brown had a more elitist feel to their campuses, but Bucknell had some clear differences among students and I knew I was on the lower end of the apparent socio-economic scale.

In addition to my social standing, a letter awaited me in my student mailbox from the academic dean's office. The letter highly recommended that I receive academic support for college. Whereas I had excelled in my high school academic work, the message for me was that I would not succeed at Bucknell. I was receiving extensive scholarship that depended upon my academic success. I perceived this as an implicit threat requiring my need for diligent work to remain at college. I knew how to compete in a large Brooklyn high school, but Bucknell was a new setting. I did not seek out the academic support during my freshman year. I suppose I surprised folk by being appointed to Phi Alpha Chi, the Freshmen Honorary Society, for my grades, whereas Brian later flunked out.

Actually I met other freshman from lower middle class backgrounds who were first-generation college students in their families. Karl Marchenese, who lived down the hall, shared a similar study ethic and desire to succeed. His goal was to go to medical school, which he achieved. We became roommates during our sophomore year. Karl was a wrestler for the school and I was amazed by the discipline of his making weight for matches. Both Karl and I did limited socializing that first year because of our intense study commitments, which resulted in good grades.

The one exception for me was to attend meetings of the Inter-Varsity (IV) Christian Fellowship, which had just launched on campus. It was a distinctly evangelical group as compared with the campus Christian student group. It emphasized the need for reasoned faith and small-group Bible studies with peers. A local Presbyterian church had prayed for years for such a launch, which began with the support of Rev. Richard Merritt and Mrs. Mayetta Christensen who recently lost her husband and eldest son in a tragic auto accident just before they were to move out west for a teaching position that fall. Having just made a personal faith commitment in the summer, I came to campus with many religious and spiritual questions that the Inter-Varsity chapter welcomed.

One of the older students, Terry, who was visually challenged, invited David Vassar, freshman football star who played fullback and me to attend a Regular Baptist Church in nearby Northumberland. He identified it as "biblically sound" and his church emphasized a fundamentalist theological stance that stressed evangelism of all those who were not born again. We were driven to church by Mr. Hackenburg who worked on the college's building and grounds crew and modeled loving care of his wife who was wheelchair bound. Her body was twisted with severe rheumatoid arthritis and she weighed all of eighty pounds, but she faithfully attended church each week, assisted by her husband with three college students in tow. With all of her pain and suffering, Mrs. Hackenburg radiated a joyful faith and genuine care for us in the midst of her pain. Over time the exclusionary and judgmental stance of the Regular Baptists alienated me from their brand of Christian faith, but I gained much from the biblical literacy they passed along—less their interpretations.

Mrs. Christensen adopted me into her family, especially after I returned to campus during my sophomore year with new responsibilities. At the close of my freshman year, I was somehow elected as the vice-president of the IV chapter. The president was a football player had flunked out, so I became the president. Mrs. Christensen, with all of her challenges as a widow with three surviving children, opened her home for weekend meals to support the now growing IV chapter. She had attended Moody Bible Institute and loved people and sharing her Christian faith with them. I too came from a family with four children, and in my case, the oldest son died, leaving me a legacy for the next male to assume. Mayetta discipled me by modeling of a committed and gracious Christian life invested in serving others. Her model reinforced the examples of my parents.

Along with my campus life, I was totally committed to my relationship with Wanda, who was now more than a girlfriend by being "pinned" with Bucknell's jewelry. Many hours were spent writing letters and cards and waiting for an open phone in the telephone room, as a host of students called their loved ones on Sunday evenings. Sunday evenings had the cheapest phone rates supported by my piles of quarters and a few dimes and nickels when needed.

Wanda had attended Ottawa University in Kansas for one semester, but returned to New York to find employment at Chase Manhattan Bank in the Wall Street area as a teletype operator. She witnessed the construction of what became the Twin Towers, which were later destroyed on 9/11 when our daughter Rebekah was in her first year at Columbia College, located just seven miles from ground zero.

Wanda and I were married between my junior and senior years on August 16, 1969. We lived in the small town of Winfield, Pennsylvania, four miles south of the Bucknell campus. At our cute, rented cottage home we had weekly IV small group meetings for prayer and Bible study. Members of the group included Tim Keller, now a nationally known pastor and author, and Jim Cummings, our friend.

One fateful Saturday morning Tim and Jim surprised Wanda and I with a visit. We just happened to be sharing a bath together as newlyweds.

I said to Wanda, "I think someone is in the house downstairs."

"No, it couldn't be. I would be too embarrassed!" she replied.

"Let me go check."

While drenched and draped in a towel, I ventured a peek down the stairs.

"Hello. Anybody there?" I queried.

"Hi, Bob!" was Tim's reply as I spied his broad smile peering up.

He inquired, "What are you and Wanda doing upstairs?"

"We are taking a bath together! What a surprise to have you visit!"

Tim's budding pastoral wisdom was: "You know bathing together like that is banned in some states!" He was always the comedian.

Wanda worked at Moore Business Forms as we adjusted to married life while a war in Vietnam filled the news, along with the Selective Service Draft held on December 1, 1969. The hated draft and issues of the war crested over the campus and led in the spring semester of 1970 to a student strike protesting the nation's war commitments. All-campus demonstrations and speak-outs were held where all views were heard. The IV chapter composed its own statement, calling for a Christian response of peace during an evident town/gown clash emerging over political differences. Many of the town's families had its members in military service and they objected to the privileged views espoused from the cloistered campus perspective.

My draft number was 180, which in most parts of the country was safe, but not in Brooklyn. I opted to explore enlisting as a Navy medic given my reluctance to bear arms in the war. (Mrs. Ferguson's lyric change from Sunday School bore fruit.) I went to the Navy recruiting office in Sudbury, PA.

"It is great to hear of your interest in the Navy. Tell me a little about yourself."

"I am a senior at Bucknell University majoring in psychology and about to graduate this May. I was married back in August and am living in Winfield. My dad served in the Army back in World War II and I thought I would volunteer rather than be drafted to serve."

"Son, congratulations on being married, but do tell me if there is anything in the oven?"

I was dumbfounded. "Anything in the oven? What in the world did he mean?"

Finally, it dawned on me. "Yes, we just learned that my wife is pregnant with our first child."

"OK, but you will need to have your physical first before we can proceed with enlistment."

In reporting for my physical in Harrisburg, I learned that an asthma attack I had just after returning to Pennsylvania in August 1969 would disqualify me from service. The medical director of Bucknell just happened to be at the emergency room at the

Lewisburg Hospital when I was being treated after a desperate late-night drive. Wanda could not manage the stick-shift Ford Fairlane 500 that Ivan Pagan had gifted us at our wedding. That summer I had worked as an outreach worker for the New York Bible Society at Rockaway Beach and had not needed to take my usual allergy medicine. We returned to our first home together in Winfield at the height of the pollen season, which resulted in the terrifying asthma attack. I had not had such an attack since the age of five and have never had another since 1969.

When I returned to New York City after my college gradua-tion, the physical I had in Pennsylvania did not prevent me from being drafted and called me to appear for the requisite physical in Brooklyn at Fort Hamilton. After the documents were reviewed from the emergency room visit and statements from Bucknell's medical firector, I was classified "1Y" and deemed unfit to serve in the military.

My initial interest in geology waned and I began to study reli-gion instead. With my religious interest I explored religion courses that became a minor study area. With the need to declare a major at the mid-point of my sophomore year, I opted for psychology. Psychology is a social science and it offered a way to better under-stand and help people. People with all of their variety and char-acteristics fascinated me, especially in exploring small-town life as compared to the city. Helping people in their life journeys also made sense from a faith perspective. I could be a Christian clini-cal psychologist just like Clyde Narramore, whom I heard on the radio! He helped folk and related his advice to the Christian faith. Here was a way to integrate my academic and spiritual interests in a life's vocation.

The professor who most influenced me through his teaching was Douglas Sturm, who taught religion. He wore dark-framed glasses that contrasted with his blonde hair. When he questioned students, Professor Sturm's eyes would widen in hope that his peering might open the remote crevices of our minds. He was an intimidating presence who expected well-prepared students to engage in Socratic dialogue with our assigned readings. We all entered class with our eyes sheepishly lowered, avoiding any contact with our professor's penetrating gaze. We thought to ourselves, "Who is today's victim of Professor Sturm's questioning?" We only relaxed if we were not the first appointed for his interrogation, which could last for half the class hour.

One memorable exchange Professor Sturm had with another student is etched on my academic memory. The student came to class fresh from a psychology course where I also heard the Freudian analysis proposed that all straight lines suggest a male's penis and all circular lines a female's vagina. Here were impressionable insights for undergraduates preoccupied with sex. The student sought to inform our religion professor of this key insight for his own work.

"Professor Sturm, do you realize that in all your markings on the chalkboard in this course, that every straight line you draw represents a male's sexual organ and every curved line, a female's sexual organ?"

"Mr. Smith, thank you for your insight shared for all to assess. But please do tell us all, what other kind of line do you propose I draw that is not either straight or curved?"

We all waited for an answer that never came.

Professor Sturm continued: "Well, with no response from Mr. Smith to my question, let us all proceed with today's required reading."

All of the undergraduates present attempted to control our laughter while opening our books and avoiding our professor's gaze.

Over time I appreciated the analysis his questioning invited us to consider in extracting the best from any text. At the close of my college years and after three courses with him, Professor Sturm met me in his office with a recommendation:

"Robert, you have completed excellent work in religious ethics and Christian thought while here at Bucknell. You should consider seminary for further study, and in particular, I recommend Union Seminary in New York. If I am not mistaken, aren't you from New York?"

"Yes, from Brooklyn and thank you for the recommendation, but I think I want to become a clinical psychologist. I certainly have enjoyed studying with you while at Bucknell."

I quickly dismissed his suggestion and that of peers from campus who also thought I should opt for seminary education.

"Paz, with so many of us considering seminary from our IV chapter, you ought to consider Gordon-Conwell, a school that Rev. Merritt recommends for us after his experience at Princeton Seminary."

"No way, not me!"

Five years later I was entering Gordon-Conwell Theological Seminary in Massachusetts (where Tim also attended) for a Master of Divinity degree, and immediately after that degree I attended Columbia University in cooperation with Union Seminary for doctoral studies in religious education. The insights of Professor Sturm and peers bore fruit.

After leaving Brooklyn a boy in 1966, I returned to New York in 1970 a married man about to become a father. Wanda and I lived with her mom at 1219 Rosedale Avenue in the Soundview section of the Bronx before moving after two years to our own apartment within a three-block distance. After a desperate search over the summer, I found full-time employment at New York Hospital/Cornell Medical Center in Whiteplains working as a crisis counselor for emotionally disturbed children. These children were headed to residential treatment facilities, but the hospital under pressure from the city government offered services to the local community in a day hospital. The children selected had some family vestiges that offered hope of an eventual return to public school with our intervention. In many cases, this was what happened. Here was an ideal setting to explore my interest in clinical psychology and to make a difference in the lives of some children and their families who struggled to survive.

Lessons Learned

Life brings unexpected turns and changes. Sharing one's life with a partner and their extended family is a blessing that I have enjoyed for over forty-seven years. The support and modeling of many persons sustains a life through times of transition. One should heed the feedback of others who know and love us when considering what life paths to explore.

Conclusion

Manna Revisted

My life represents a tapestry woven together in the country of Brooklyn. Peter Golenbock identifies Brooklyn as a country unto itself in his work *In the Country of Brooklyn: Inspiration to the World.* Urban legend has it that one in every seven people living in the United States has a personal or familial connection with Brooklyn.

The strength, cohesion, and complementarity of families, neighborhoods, churches, and schools influence the formation of children and youth. Without an effective educational ecology, a sense of hopelessness and even rage can emerge and gang culture can flourish. Children need security and consistency and buffering institutions that serve to mitigate the impacts of economic, political, and social downturns. Such downturns can sabotage childhood dreams, visions, and hopes for a meaningful and productive life. Personal choices must be considered, but limited choices for life paths influence life trajectories and the exploration of alternatives to those subtle messages given to those who grew up on the wrong side of defining avenues, like Bedford Avenue in Brooklyn.

The mentoring and nurturing roles of key adults are both informative and formative for children, while we still recognize from a religious perspective the need for transformative encounters that affirm one's significance as a child of God deserving of unconditional love and called to serve others.

Recounting a singular life journey invites celebration of learning from others. Reviewing memories of my boyhood in Brooklyn has helped me to see the tapestry of life gifted to each of us. My lens for viewing my past is shaped by being a professor of education fascinated with how lessons are passed across the generations. My lens is shaped by being a person of faith. Therefore my recounting takes the form of an educational memoir that embraces my multifaceted Christian identity. Brooklyn, known as the borough of churches, has shaped the lives of millions over the years and my recounting reflects one story among many.

My daughter, though born and raised outside of Boston, Massachusetts, now resides in Brooklyn and hopes to never leave it. After graduating from Columbia University, where I completed doctoral study, she attended Brooklyn Law School and continues to live in the Brooklyn Heights neighborhood as a practicing attorney. The love of Brooklyn continues for my family.

My memoir, educational in character, has discussed the key influences of my life, nurtured in Brooklyn and shared over my career through publications in the field of religious education. This volume adds to those publications a personal reflection on the lessons learned from a boyhood spent in Brooklyn. More than a gift to my grandchildren, I pray my writing will bless many people. My life has been blessed with memories worth sharing. Being different isn't being deficient and my Brooklyn roots affirmed this lesson. As an educator, I have shared specific lessons learned from my childhood. Prayerfully, they can help others as I pass them on.

Exodus 16:32 records how God asked Moses to store up two quarts of manna because God wanted future generations to see the food that sustained folk in the desert. In verse 33 of that chapter, Moses tells Aaron: "Put some manna in a jar and store it in the place of worship for future generations to see." This is my prayer for my readers, a memoir as my treasured jar.